It is a very big honor to be friends with such a great man of God as Pastor Bob Larson. He is one of the few people who really understands the spiritual causes of many problems in the lives of people. Many difficulties that pastors and leaders face in their marriages are connected to the undercover Spirit of Jezebel. Pastor Bob's book, *Jezebel—Defeating Your #1 Spiritual Enemy*, exposes this evil spirit and shows the way to defeat it!

Pastor Bob Larson is always a big blessing for all New Generation Churches, not only in Ukraine and Europe, but also in Russia. He has an amazing gift to bring the audience into the realm of the spiritual world during his meetings. With great pleasure I suggest that everyone read Pastor Bob's new book: *Jezebel—Defeating Your #1 Spiritual Enemy*.

—ANDREY TISCHENKO
Senior Bishop of more than 300 New Generation Churches
in Ukraine, Europe, and Russia
Founder and President of the largest Bible College in Eastern
Europe, New Generation Bible College, Ukraine
Board Member of Church Growth International, President
Dr. Yonggi Cho

JEZEBEL

JEZEBEL

DEFEATING YOUR #1 SPIRITUAL ENEMY

BOB LARSON

DESTINY IMAGE® PUBLISHERS, INC.

P.O. Box 310, Shippensburg, PA 17257-0310

"Promoting Inspired Lives."

This book and all other Destiny Image and Destiny Image Fiction books are available at Christian bookstores and distributors worldwide.

Cover and interior design by Terry Clifton

For more information on foreign distributors, call 717-532-3040.

Or reach us on the Internet: www.destinyimage.com

ISBN 13: HC 978-0-7684-1303-8

ISBN 13: TP 978-0-7684-0706-8

ISBN 13 EBook: 978-0-7684-0707-5

For Worldwide Distribution, Printed in the U.S.A.

1 2 3 4 5 6 7 8 9 10 11 / 18 17 16 15

Dedication

TO MY FAMILY

THIS BOOK IS DEDICATED TO MY FAMILY: MY WIFE LAURA AND OUR three daughters. It is not the first book I have dedicated to them, but this time is special. Our daughters are now young women, facing a world in which the spirit of Jezebel is running amok, in both society and the Church. All credit is due to my wife for raising them to be young women of honor and integrity, no small feat in these times. In my personal counseling and deliverance ministry I encounter almost daily those who are afflicted by Jezebel through their own actions or the conduct of those who have influenced them, especially parents. The steadfastness of my family is especially commendable because my ministry responsibilities have often taken me to distant places for considerable lengths of time. My family has made the writing of this book possible by their understanding and faithful love for the Lord.

Jezebel's name has been used for thousands of years to describe cunning, ruthless and reprehensible women. Some believe she typifies evil. She became known for putting on makeup before her death and being a wicked woman.
—BIOGRAPHY CHANNEL

But there was no one like Ahab who sold himself to do wickedness in the sight of the Lord, because Jezebel his wife stirred him up.
—1 KINGS 21:25

And concerning Jezebel the Lord also spoke, saying, "The dogs shall eat Jezebel by the wall of Jezreel."
—1 KINGS 21:23

So they threw her down, and some of her blood spattered on the wall and on the horses; and he trampled her underfoot.... So they went to bury her but they found no more of her than the skull and the feet and the palms of her hands.
—2 KINGS 9:33, 35 (843 BC)

CONTENTS

Introduction

JEZEBEL, AGENT OF CONTROL, MANIPULATION, MURDER—ENEMY OF THE CHRISTIAN CHURCH

*Nevertheless I have a few things against you, because
you allow that woman Jezebel, who calls herself a
prophetess, to teach and seduce my servants to commit
sexual immorality and eat things sacrificed to idols.*
—REVELATION 2:20
(message from the angel of the church in Thyatira)

"WHAT DEMON DO YOU DEAL WITH THE MOST?"

Members of the media have asked me that question a thousand
times, maybe more. Every time the lights are set, the cameras in place,
sound checks completed, and the scene slated, it's the one inquiry posed
by almost every journalist and TV commentator.

Certainly they ask other questions: "How long have you been doing
this?" (Nearly four decades.) "How many exorcisms have you done?"

(30,000 plus, and counting, documented cases.) "What was your most notable case?" (They are always looking for the spinning heads and green-pea vomit.)

Then, "Which demon do you meet more than any other?"

I've been interviewed for radio, TV, and screen so many times the answers are mostly easy. This answer is really easy—"Jezebel."

Most reporters have heard the name. Who hasn't? It conjures images of some hussy, a harlot, an adulterous kind of female character. To call a woman a Jezebel is to evoke images of seduction, cleavage, come-hither glances, and sexual fascination. Sure that's Jezebel, but that's also missing that point. Jezebel is so much more. More intrigue, guile, and deception. As you'll soon learn, Jezebel isn't a one-dimensional character lifted from a pulp-fiction romance novel or a grade-B erotic flick. Jezebel is sophisticated, cunning, and, above all, *religious*.

Twenty-two times Jezebel is mentioned in the Bible, all but one in First and Second Kings. Her wicked husband, Ahab, is referred to more than 90 times. Surely with such ubiquitous attention this ancient monarch of murder deserves more than casual allusions. And as an exorcist who has been credited by the international press with having done more exorcisms than anyone on the planet, my observations should bear some weight.

Why such pervasiveness? Is Jezebel's heightened activity the result of inordinate attention, overblown by attempts to simplify allusions to evil by using one provocative name? Or is the prevalence of Jezebel indicative of the times in which we live? Is this demonic force prophetically significant of the apocalyptic end of the ages?

Why *do* I meet Jezebel the most? The answer to that question is on the pages that follow. You'll meet this evil identity head-on, though you've likely met her before and didn't know it. You'll discover her role in pop culture, relationships, marriages, and even the Christian Church. She's in the Bible, but you already probably know that. Who is she now, today, in everyday life? What do you do if you meet her? Run? Dodge? Fight?

There are certain archetypes of evil that resonate with humanity from other ages: Herod, Nero, Attila; closer to our age Hitler, Stalin, Pol Pot. But none compares to the dynamic duo of Jezebel and her marital accomplice Ahab: "Now Ahab the son of Omri did evil in the sight of the Lord, more than all who were before him" (1 Kings 16:30).

In this book you will meet the embodiment of ultimate evil. You'll be shocked at how duplicitous Jezebel can be, how cleverly she has infiltrated even the most sacrosanct of places. Mostly you'll be stunned at how Jezebel has hidden right under your own nose, in the life of someone you care about and spiritual leaders you have respected. To describe her presence, one might cry out, "She's everywhere; she's everywhere."

Everywhere, indeed. And all the while provoking discord and jealousy, fanning lust and degeneracy, inciting piousness and perversion. Once you meet her in all of her perfidy, you will not like what you see. But you'll be glad the veil on her evil has been lifted so that you will be able to recognize her the next time she enters your world on a spiritual search-and-destroy mission.

Jezebel—who she is and what she does—we are about to expose her for all her evil.

You may be surprised to learn that, in this hour of human history, she is your *#1 spiritual enemy*.

Special Note: Angels whenever seen in vision or human form always biblically appear as male, though their celestial estate can't be compared to our human definitions of sexuality (see Matt. 22:30). Therefore, it can be assumed that the demonic manifestation of Jezebel, a male demon, may for the purposes of evil appear in feminine form. In this book, when the pronouns "she" or "her" are used in reference to Jezebel as an evil spirit they should not be taken as a literal gender identification. Female pronouns will be employed as a literary device referencing the "female" activity and intent of Jezebel as a fallen angel.

Chapter 1

A Phoenician
Princess Reigns

I'd know that look anywhere. The arched eyebrows. The askance gaze of seductive taunting. The come-hither-but-don't-approach intensity. The slight smirk of arrogance and diabolical charm. I'd seen it before in music videos, on the movie and TV screen, and gracing the covers of hundreds of magazines. It was an unmistakable stare. In a micro-second it said both, "I'll outwit you," and "I'm more powerful than you." Then she spoke.

"You again!"

"Yes, me again. You remember?"

That smirk again. "Of course, how could I forget? But this time I win. Leanna wants me. I'm so much a part of her that this woman doesn't know what's her and what's me. Clever, huh?"

"But not clever enough for the Holy Spirit."

"She likes what I do for her. So many things she can't do for herself."

"But once she understands that it's you, a demon, doing it, she'll change her mind," I countered.

The smugness turned to anger. "I hate you!"

"I'd be worried if you liked me," I responded.

"Humph! We'll see. First you'll have to convince her that I'm evil. She thinks I'm her friend, Marianna. And she doesn't even know who Marianna is."

At that point I wasn't certain who Marianna was, either. A fragmented, mind-altering personality? A demon by some other name? Someone that abused Leanna and was soul bonded to her mind? An ancestral memory from past generations? From the thousands of cases like this I knew it could be any of the above. That's when Jezebel in her hubris tripped up. She offered me information that would have been hard to find otherwise. Jezebel should have kept quiet, but her pride got the best of her.

"We've had her bloodline for 15 generations. This woman has no idea what happened. Babies! Blood! All sacrificed to me. This curse is too long and too strong to break. There are too many of us. We are legion, and we own her soul!"

I laughed out loud. "Heard that one before," I retorted. "Demons like you always want to convince me they are 'Legion,' to intimidate. I'm not buying that. Nothing is too strong for God."

Jezebel's look was no longer beguiling. "Her father was into metaphysics. He read dark books. Oh, add to that—her aunt was a witch. People came to her to have their cards read. She was good at it, too. And this woman? She invited us when she bought that Tibetan prayer wheel on the Internet. Clever, don't you think? She was told it would bring her closer to God."

I listened. There's a big difference between letting a demon ramble to draw it into the open versus unwisely allowing it to brag. This time Jezebel's self-conceit had gotten the best of her. "Witchcraft, lots of it, all through the bloodline. Why else do you think she was drawn to the New Age? But the worst thing that happened to her was her abuse. Molested at five. I was there making sure it happened."

"Marianna?" I inquired drawing out Jezebel further on a limb.

"Oh yes, Marianna, the ancient one who still lives on in her mind. She was ritually raped. I was there, I watched when it happened. All to Baal. And Moloch, naturally."

Jezebel was almost casual in recounting Leanna's ancestry. Then suddenly, the demon switched and became intense. "I've told you too much! No one is supposed to know all this. Especially not you."

My spiritual strategy had paid off. Diabolically ingenious though she was, Jezebel had succumbed to her own cockiness and told far more than she normally would have. Procedurally, from the standpoint of an exorcism, the path had been laid out before me. Bring resolution to the inherited soul fragment of Marianna, minister healing to the wounded part of Leanna who had suffered abuse as a child, cancel the generational curses of witchcraft and blood sacrifice, and get Leanna to renounce her own occultism. Once we completed that, Jezebel's power would be broken.

It wasn't easy. Hours of prayer and wrestling with Jezebel and her satanic cohorts followed. They didn't give up without a fight. The deliverance process took enough twists and turns it could have been fodder for a soap opera script. But eventually, all the elements of freeing Leanna were dealt with. Every spiritual technicality by which Jezebel claimed a right to Leanna was carefully processed by prayer. Now, it was down to expelling Jezebel.

"I'll be back," the demon bragged. "She doesn't know how to live without me. I'm like Janus, the two-headed god. One side is her and the other me."

That's how Jezebel works; embedding in the victim's mind and emotions to the extent that the evil is barely detectable. Unless cornered and confronted, Jezebel works in stealth more than any evil spirit I've exorcised. Hide, duck, conceal—Jezebel does it well; embellish with spirituality, especially feigned godliness. Remember, John the Revelator warned us that she comes as a prophetess, concealing her true motives. What better way to destroy the work of God than by infiltrating at the highest ranks of spiritual leadership. Preachers, teachers, deacons, elders, men, women, from the pulpit to the pastor's home.

As the end of Leanna's exorcism unfolded, Jezebel changed her tune. "I'll make a deal," she bargained. "I'll go. Just let me enter someone else. There are so many who want me."

"The Pit, Jezebel, that's where you're going," I insisted.

The demon screamed. "No! Not the Abyss. I'll go anywhere but there!"

"Plus you're taking Witchcraft, Baal, and Moloch with you," I insisted.

Jezebel's grimace turned into a groan. Hours of prayer were about to bear fruit, but not without a battle. A scrape on my arm still oozed blood from where Jezebel had dug in Leanna's nails before I could react. My right leg still throbbed from a well-placed kick from Jezebel, before those assisting me could respond quickly enough to restrain the demon. But any injury was minor compared with God's judgement that Jezebel was about to receive.

"Just to make sure that you go and never come back, I call the dogs of Jezreel to come now, and eat your flesh and lick your blood."

The scream that ensued was so loud it pained my ears. Jezebel was in torment

"Here they come now. Hear them yelping?"

Then I added a biblical allusion. "Look over your shoulder Jezebel, the eunuchs are in the window about to throw you to the street below." I held Leanna's forearm tightly and lifted the palm of her hand in Jezebel's face. "This is all that will be left of you. Just your hands and your skull!"

My actions were more than scriptural melodrama. I was declaring spiritual truth and directing it supernaturally into the spirit world as an actualized reality to Jezebel.

I could have opened a Bible and read Second Kings chapter nine, but that would have been superfluous. This demon knew full well the story of Jezebel's end as Queen of Israel and instigator of Baal worship, and how her body was thrown down in the streets of Jezreel to be eaten by the dogs and trampled by horses. Nothing was left save her skull, hands, and feet. I was taking this Old Testament account of a literal event and applying it spiritually to this hideous evil spirit. The effect of literalizing God's word in such a direct way was powerful. Jezebel shrieked in terror and begged to avoid Jehovah's judgment.

What a change from the audacity displayed in the beginning of Leanna's exorcism. In moments this despicable demon had repeated the words, "I go, now, to the Pit!" and exited with convulsions, while thrashing about with screeches of fright.

Jezebel was gone—from Leanna. But I knew that other Jezebels were in waiting, prepared to do battle in another place and time. (Jezebel isn't a single demon. Like evil spirits such as those named Lucifer, Satan, Beelzebub etc., certain demons acquire nominal generic designations, "brand" names which indicate they have risen to such a level of evil that they qualify for this honorific ranking.) The circumstances might be different in the future, but the struggle with Jezebel would be similar. I've learned from casting out thousands of Jezebel demons (more than any other, as I have already noted) that there is a cadence to encounters with this demon who is named after that wicked woman from nearly 3,000 years ago.

Now that you've met Jezebel up close and personal, let's delve deeper into the spiritual psyche of this emblem of evil and wanton wickedness. In the following chapters you'll meet all the characters of this classic battle between good and evil, complete with political skullduggery, murderous plots, and the titanic confrontation between Jezebel's false religion of Baal worship and the austere, but bold, prophet of God named Elijah. The story of Jezebel has it all. Sex, intrigue, religious apostasy, nefarious schemes, fraud, treason, and tragedy.

OLD TESTAMENT QUEEN

Jezebel presided over one of history's most brutal empires, built on human blood. Cunning, ruthless, powerful, Jezebel still lives on as the archetype of "liberated" womanhood, despoiled and fearsome. How did this Phoenician princess become the queen to King Ahab, ruling over all Israel?

When Ahab was crowned king, Israel sought an alliance with its northern, more cosmopolitan, neighbor Phoenicia. The daughter of King Ethbaal, king of the Zidonians, Jezebel had likely been groomed to be an intermediary between her own pagan kingdom and the people of God. The marriage of Jezebel and Ahab turned what had been a Jewish/Phoenician international competition into accommodation and compromise instead of rivalry. For the first time, a king of Israel had joined in marriage with a heathen. Disaster was to follow

This unholy alliance was to be Israel's eventual undoing. Jezebel played the role of political consort well by bringing along 850 of her Baal prophets to replace the worship of Yahweh, eventually murdering several Jewish prophets. For the first time in Israel's history, there was a great, organized, "official" persecution of those faithful to God. Jezebel was unrestrained in her hatred for the religious piety of the people over whom she reigned. Idolatry, in all its Phoenician splendor, now dominated the religious tenor of the Jewish kingdom. This new religion of Baal worship also brought with it the basest kinds of practices: sensual temple prostitution, licentious rituals, and infanticide.

It is clear from the Bible that this Phoenician interloper was not content to sit on a throne and play second fiddle to her husband. She brought with her from her own country all the accoutrements of the witchcraft of her culture. It had to be obvious to religious Israelites that the entire country was turning away from the reason for their existence—their connection to the one true god, Jehovah.

The result was God's judgment of a drought and famine, predicted by the godly prophet Elijah. For three years it did not rain. Then true to the character of Jezebel, the woman and the demon, opposition and judgment from God only hardened her attitude. (I've seen this stubborn demeanor many times in the demons that bear her name.) This led to that pivotal confrontation on Mount Carmel between the prophet of God and the priests of Baal. (We shall speak more of this later to demonstrate that, even in the face of religious humiliation, Jezebel was not deterred from her devotion to the demon gods of her homeland.)

Finally, things came to a head in the fight over a vineyard, owned by one Naboth. Ahab wanted Naboth's vineyard and subordinated his desires to Jezebel who hatched a plot to have Naboth charged with blasphemy and executed. The scheme worked, as we'll explore in another chapter, and Ahab got what he wanted; but this brought Jezebel closer to God's ultimate judgment.

In the end Jezebel arrogantly attempted one last time to seduce her executioner Jehu by applying the best of her finery, enhanced by cosmetic skills. Jezebel dressed for death and put on her makeup before being cast down in ignominy. She had "painted" herself into a corner of destruction in the most horrible fashion—stomped by horses and eaten by dogs. Subsequently her name became a synonym for all that is base and treacherous. Because of her ruthlessness, she has typified evil at its worst for thousands of years.

Ironically, Jezebel has some apologists today who see her as the first bra-burner, a feminist caught unfairly in a political struggle for control over religion and thus an empire; the first "suffragette." Was Jezebel a misunderstood, independent woman living in patriarchal times and taking a bad rap for challenging the system? Who was Jezebel and what has the historical character to do with the demon claiming this name?

The key question we must resolve is this: Is Jezebel more than a curious character shrouded in ancient stories and legend as the personification of feminine sorcery and seduction? Has her evil been magnified repeatedly throughout history through her adaptations as other idolatrous entities, such as Venus and Diana? Is Jezebel an active agency today as a demonic identity seeking to enslave those who yield to her seduction? The answers lie ahead on these pages.

Chapter 2

LILITH IN HER MANY FORMS

Clouds glowered on the horizon. Eden had not seen this before. Perhaps that should have been a clue to Eve that something was amiss. But she was so focused on the fruit that she hardly noticed.

The serpent certainly did. He was all too aware that an epic encounter was about to take place. He wasn't alone. All those who had fallen with him watched, from their various perspectives in the atmosphere. This Garden, this glorious refuge of peace and plentifulness, had been untouched by the fall from Heaven's grace. As the sun glinted reflectively from the Deceiver's eyes, he knew that some measure of revenge was about to be extracted. If only he could convince her. Just one bite. That's all he needed. Summoning all the subtlety his evil intent could muster, he argued, "Are you sure that's what God said? You really mustn't eat of that Tree of the Knowledge of Good and Evil?"

Behind the Evil One, a hideous presence smirked, a taunting look that chilled even the most hardened ones in hell. It was Lilith. Consort, of sorts, of Lucifer. Not just any reprehensible entity, the One. The yin to Satan's yang. True, there was only maleness in the divine scheme of the supernatural. All the unfallen ones were created that way. They had no aspirations to femaleness. It was unknown. But now that this beautiful companion known as Eve had come forth from Adam's side, the hounds of hell realized that their strategy must evolve. Some of them must take on her form. They must strive to take on all her qualities of sensuousness and delicateness. Mimic the first woman, even perhaps supplant her? That scheme could unfold later. What mattered now was that bite. That first sweet taste of the forbidden, and then—could Lucifer and Lilith even contemplate the possibility—Adam too would partake. That would compete the transaction of nefarious damnation.

As of yet there was no Other to worship, only Him. Adam and Eve had known nothing but His presence, His companionship, His creative impulse. But all that was about to change if only Eve would eat. It was the Deceiver who spoke, but it was Lilith who provoked. The ancient Scriptures would not speak of her until later, but she was there helping to orchestrate each step, looking for a way to implement the human Fall and from that go forward to corrupt all that the Creator had intended for these who had been made a little lower than the angels.

When Lilith heard that first crunch, the sound of teeth and gums consuming the forbidden, she knew something horribly wicked was coming. Now, she could set in motion all the malevolency that had filled her since the great transgression that had forced her ejection from Paradise. Satan had his sights on Adam, but Lilith, in all her diabolical cunningness, focused on Eve. If Lilith could corrupt all that God had intended for Adam's Rib, her revenge against the Almighty just might be extracted in some measure. Ideas were spinning in her head. The possibility—those who could come from Adam and Eve might worship someone, or something, or than Him. And what if that someone was a being modeled after Eve? That notion held endless possibility of corrupting the divine. What if an entity purporting to have what Eve almost possessed offered it again in opposition to all that Jehovah would purpose? Lilith's cold blood surged at the idea it might be possible.

The scheme was perfect in all its evil: Posit not just Lucifer as an alternative to God, but Lilith as the true Eve. Who would know later what the truth of Eden really was if the human desire to worship could be bent toward one like Eve? Names of this grand deception coursed through the machinations of evil that was Lilith's corrupted genius. Aphrodite? Artemis? Isis? Diana? Kali? Venus? The list was endless. The potential unending. With this grand, diabolical design Lilith could seek to destroy what the Creator had intended for femaleness; she could also use this fraud to seduce all men into an alliance with the antithesis of Eve's essence.

Let the games begin!

THE MANY FORMS OF JEZEBEL

Throughout antiquity, Jezebel has been worshiped in many forms, and has been known by many names. Since the fall of humanity, Satan has sought to interject a feminine demonic principle into false worship, emphasizing a matriarchal control over societies with various manifestations of female, fertility goddesses. Among the versions of this idolatrous demonic deity are the examples that follow.

Ishtar (Babylonian)

The ancient Babylonian and Assyrian goddess Ishtar symbolized Mother Earth in the natural cycles of fertility on earth. Ishtar was the daughter of Sin, the moon god. She was the goddess of love, so the practice of ritual prostitution became widespread in the fertility cult dedicated to her name. Temples to Ishtar had many priestesses, or sacred prostitutes, who symbolically acted out the fertility rites of the cycle of nature. Ishtar has been identified with the Phoenician Astarte, the Semitic Ashtoreth, and the Sumerian Inanna. Strong similarities also exist between Ishtar and the Egyptian Isis, the Greek Aphrodite, and the Roman Venus.

Anat (Canaanite)

Baal's mistress or lover was Anat (or Anath), the goddess of war, love, and fertility. She was the virgin goddess who conceived, and was also the victor over Baal's enemies. With the help of Shapash, the sun god, Anat rescued Baal from Mot (the god of death). Her victories in battle were vicious; she is described as up to her hips in gore with heads and hands from the enemies stacked high. Thus, Anat was the driving force in the annual fertility cycle of Baal.

Anat is sometimes identified with the "queen of heaven," to whom the Jews offered incense in Jeremiah's day (see Jer. 7:18; 44:17–19, 25). But some scholars identify the "queen of heaven" with the Babylonian goddess Ishtar. Anat was the patroness of sex and passion; lewd figurines of this nude goddess have been discovered at various archaeological sites in Palestine.

Ashtoreth (Syrian/Phoenician)

Mentioned in First Kings 11:5, 33 and Second Kings 23:13, this deity was the ancient Syrian and Phoenician goddess of the moon, sexuality, sensual love, and fertility. In the Old Testament, Ashtoreth is often associated with the worship of Baal. The word *Ashtaroth* in the King James Version of the Bible is the plural form of Ashtoreth; the New King James has *Ashtoreths* (see Judg. 2:13; 1 Sam. 12:10).

Diana (Roman)/Artemis (Greek)

Referred to in Acts 19:24, 27–28, 34–35, this goddess in Roman mythology was the deity of the moon, hunting, wild animals, and virginity. Diana is the same as the Greek goddess *Artemis*, virgin goddess of the hunt and the moon. When Paul preached in Ephesus, the citizens were stirred to an uproar because the gospel threatened to destroy the profit of the artisans who crafted silver shrines of Diana.

The temple of Artemis at Ephesus was one of the seven wonders of the ancient world. The Ephesian Artemis, or Diana, was worshiped more widely by individuals than any other deity known in the Asian world. The dissemination of the cult was aided by a strong missionary zeal by its devotees as well as an annual month-long festival held in her honor.

The temple wielded tremendous power through its function as a banking and financial center. The cult also obtained a sizable income from the large amount of property owned in the environs of Ephesus. Unsurpassed cosmic power was attributed to her. To those who called upon Artemis she was Savior, Lord, and Queen of the Cosmos. She could exercise her power for the benefit of the devotee in the face of other opposing "powers" and spirits. As goddess of the underworld, she possessed authority and control over the multiplicity of demons of the dead as well as the demons of nature and of everyday life.

Aphrodite/Venus (Greek)

The most commonly accepted legend concerning the birth of Aphrodite indicates that she was born of the foam of the sea, floated in a shell on the waves, and later landed on Cyprus near Paphos. The greatest festival in Cyprus in honor of Aphrodite was the Aphrodisia, held for three days each spring. Each year great crowds attended it, not only from all parts of Cyprus but also from surrounding countries. During the Aphrodisia a religious procession started at New Paphos and wound its way to Old Paphos, some ten miles away, passing through the gardens and sanctuaries of the goddess.

Isis (Egyptian)

The Egyptians believed the dead go to a territory ruled by Osiris, where a person must give an account of his good and bad deeds. Behind this was the Osiris legend, which tells how the benevolent ruler Osiris was killed by his wicked brother Set, who cut his body into pieces. His wife, and sister, Isis, searched for his dismembered body and restored it to life. Eventually Osiris descended into the underworld as the judge of the dead. His son, Horus, avenged his father's death by killing Set. Subsequently the myth of Osiris' death and resurrection stimulated the Egyptians' hope for immortality. For Osiris, life won out over death;

good won over evil. So the Egyptians reasoned the same could happen to them.

Kali (Hindu)

In Hinduism, Kali is depicted in as an idol painted completely black with demonically bulging eyes. In one hand she holds a sword, and the other hand holds the head of her decapitated lover. Around her neck is a necklace of the human skulls of her victims. She stands with one foot triumphantly placed on back of the corpse of her murdered paramour. She is infamous for seducing her lovers and then, at the moment of orgasm, taking their lives. In India, where the cult of Kali originated, she is revered and feared by those who tremble at her sexual powers and bloodthirsty prowess.

Lilith (Witchcraft and Occult Judaism)

Mystical, Kabbalistic, and occult Judaism has taught that Adam's first wife was Lilith. She was supplanted by Eve, and consequently became an evil spirit. As Adam's true wife she seeks restoration to her rightful position. In Babylonian mythology and medieval demonology she morphed into an infamous witch and sorceress, the ultimate power of womanhood with unequaled powers of sexual deception and persuasion.

These forms of Jezebel, the permutations of evil rooted ultimately in Lilith and now known as variations on the biblical Jezebel, are certainly not the only modalities of female corruption. They are simply the best known. We'll explore others later, but for now the reader should understand that Jezebel is highly adaptable to the times and culture in which she operates. The names change, the accoutrements vary, but the essence of murder and spiritual mayhem is never altered. What purpose do these variations serve?

The diabolical ingenuity of evil often develops a matrix of wickedness that displays itself in many contingencies. Each image of the ultimate feminine evil varies according to the epoch of history, the particulars of a civilization, the unique religious instincts of that civilization, the willingness of any people to be corrupted, and the extent to which that corruption can be accomplished. Some likenesses of Lilith are quite philosophical (Aphrodite), sexualized (Ashtoreth), religious (Isis), political (Diana), and even murderous (Kali).

As a practical matter, the demons behind these occult constructs are merely looking for room to maneuver, a place to hide, and a religious rationale for sensual indulgences. Whether Egyptian, Greek, Roman, or Middle Eastern, cult worship is the focus, the ultimate purpose is the same: Disparage the patriarchy of God the Father and displace the Holy Trinity with devotion to a matriarchal-based system of worship.

Chapter 3

CONTROL FREAK

"I HEAR IN MY MIND THE WORDS, *SOMETHING HAS BEEN STOLEN*. What do you think it means?"

Most people going through the process of deliverance are somewhat passive participants. They know little about what's involved in ridding an individual of evil spirits. Their understanding is sketchy, drawn from Hollywood motifs, what they've read of an author such as me, or my YouTube-posted examples. They seldom are participatory in the process of their getting free. This woman, Ellen, was different. She could sense what was happening in her own internal spirit world.

"Well," I said, "since the demons inside you have already presented themselves before, let's make them tell us what was stolen."

With my ever-present Cross of Deliverance in one hand and a Bible in the other, I spoke with a demanding tone. "What has been stolen from this woman?"

The first sound was a growl and gnashing of teeth. Ellen's jaw clenched hard. The demon didn't want to speak. "I demand to know, what was taken?"

"Her destiny! We don't know what it is, only God knows that. But whatever it is, we've kept it from happening! We hindered every moment of her life."

"And who are you?"

"A fallen angel."

"I know that," I responded with irritation. "Your name. Tell me your name."

"Perversion. But I'm just a minion. It's my job to protect the others."

"Who is behind you?"

"I can't tell you! I open the doors. I let everyone in."

"I'm not taking 'No' for an answer. Who is the chief, the Strong Man?'

The demon cackled. "Oh, come on now. You know her. Jezebel. Why not? This woman's mother was a control freak. She had to micromanage everything. Oh yeah, she was a real Jezebel. That's why I'm here. The curse of this woman's mother set her up to be sexually abused. After the abuse she had no one to talk to. No one to help her. As a result, she started to hate all men. That's how I entered, through the hate. All because of her mother, the old Jezebel. Because of the fear and hatred of men, this woman kept to herself, isolated and alone. She never married, and never broke away from her mother. Stayed with dear ol' mom all her life, until the old bag died and we took her to hell!"

I now knew who Perversion was hiding. Ellen's mom was a Jezebel in spirit and behavior; and she passed that demon on to her daughter, sealing the deal when the molestation took place.

"Step aside, Perversion. I call up the spirit of Jezebel!"

This Jezebel spirit was no alluring seductress. She was just plain angry, mad at having her cover blown and her defensive minions brushed aside. "Yes, I stole this woman's destiny," the demon bragged. "She never knew love. Never had a family. No children. No one but me in her life."

I pressed my Bible on Ellen's head as a symbolic gesture indicating that I was submitting Jezebel to God's authority. The demon squirmed and shot back, "Get that thing off me! Don't you know? I am a master ruling spirit. I have entire kingdoms of evil under me."

"Give back her destiny," I insisted.

"That's not for me to do. That's the job of your angels. Why don't you ask them?"

I did.

"Lord," I prayed, "please send mighty angels to come now and restore what Jezebel has stolen."

"Get them away from me," Jezebel screamed. "Those swords hurt when they strike me. Tell them to stop. I hate the angels."

I didn't, of course, call off the angels. In fact, I asked the Lord to intensify the torment until this spirit was sufficiently weakened. When the time came to complete the deliverance, I commanded Jezebel to leave, in the Name of Jesus. The physical response to the demon's exit was typical: coughing, gagging, contortions, and finally, relief. Jezebel seldom makes a quiet egress.

When Ellen collected her senses and came back to reality, we reflected on what had been learned. Every exorcism is an education in spiritual warfare, and this deliverance was particularly instructive. Ellen's demonic bondage was affected considerably by the circumstances of her life. Jezebel was in her mother and this gave a spiritual legal right leading to Ellen's demonic inhabitation. (Family dynamics often play a key role leading to spiritual oppression.) Almost all of Ellen's existence had been orchestrated with a wave of Jezebel's baton. Control, control, control. That's Jezebel, all right.

To understand this further, let's return to the biblical account of Jezebel and see what we can learn about the modus operandi depicted in the account of Naboth's stolen vineyard. We've already explained how the historical Jezebel came to reign over Israel, but her actions, once she was enthroned, are revealing.

In Jezreel, the very city where Jezebel was to meet her end eventually, a beautiful vineyard could be found, owned by a man named Naboth the Jezreelite. Unfortunately, it was near to one of Ahab's palaces. Ahab approached Naboth, offering to buy the vineyard in some form of commerce. (Money, in the sense of coins, was not yet part of Israelite culture.) Naboth's response was instant. There was no "I'll think it over." Refusing to sell was not a matter of price or condition: "The Lord forbid that I should give the inheritance of my fathers to you" (1 Kings 21:3).

This wasn't an issue of stubbornness but of spiritual principle. Naboth had not been seduced by Jezebel's introduction of Baal worship. He clung to the ways of his family whose devotion was toward the God of Israel. To sell the vineyard to Ahab, or to anyone for that matter, would be a violation of Mosaic Law. His refusal was not a display of disdain to the king's wishes, a mere sentiment of stubbornness. Naboth was duty-bound by God to keep the land in his family. But such religious formalities meant nothing to Ahab.

As of yet, the woman Jezebel was not aware of the proposed transaction. But the demon Jezebel did know what was happening and saw Naboth's ancestral respect as an opening for mischief. The moment that Ahab returned to his palace, depressed and sullen over Naboth's rebuff, the spirit of Jezebel kicked into action. As we might put it in the vernacular today, Ahab retired to his bed, pulled the covers over his head, and sulked. He refused to eat. Jezebel saw her husband's behavior and learned of the cause. Her reaction was immediate. Demons waste no time when they see an opportunity.

Inspired by the evil spirits within her, the queen declared, in so many words, "Why should you pout like this. You're the king and can have anything you want. I've no idea why you want this particular vineyard, but that's beside the point. You want it, take it. And if you don't, I will. Get up and eat. Be merry. I'll handle this. Naboth's vineyard is as good as yours."

The Bible doesn't tell us how long this situation germinated in Jezebel's thoughts as she hatched a plot. The sense is that she acted posthaste.

In First Kings 21, between verse seven which records Jezebel saying "I will give you the vineyard" and verse eight ("And she wrote letters...") there is nothing. The sense is that she was swift.

My experience with the demon Jezebel informs me that this demon is ingenious and impulsive. The plot to take the vineyard required little connivance. It was as if the entire scheme popped full-blown into the queen's mind. She would write letters, sealed with the king's own signet, and thus invite all the key leaders of Israel to the king's court of Samaria, about seven miles from Jezreel. The missive to all the nobles and elders read as follows:

> *Proclaim a fast, and seat Naboth with high honor among the people; and seat two men, scoundrels, before him to bear witness against him, saying, You have blasphemed God and the king. Then take him out, and stone him, that he may die* (1 Kings 21:9–10).

In this simple, diabolic instruction is a wealth of information about how Jezebel operates.

HOW THE JEZEBEL SPIRIT FUNCTIONS

- *Jezebel isn't usually subtle, only ruthless.* The actions to follow are straightforward. Any pretense about the real purpose of this kangaroo court is set aside. Jezebel acts decisively. Naboth is to be tried and condemned. The outcome is a foregone conclusion.

- *Jezebel appeals to religious sentiments.* A fast was proclaimed. There was a pretense of spiritual solemnity. That's often Jezebel's cover. She comes in priestly robes, religious language, and feigned spiritual motives.

- *Jezebel shifts the blame.* Though Jezebel is putting a curse on Naboth, she accuses him of the crime of cursing God and the king. The alleged wrongdoing is that Naboth, at some undesignated time conjured only in the mind of Jezebel, cursed God. Clever. Jezebel, in reality, is the one cursing a godly man, but the evil she does is what Naboth is blamed for. There is no lack of Jezebel's evil ingenuity when ascribing bad motives to the people of God, especially spiritual leaders: "They're in it for the money," or "He/she isn't really sincere, it's all an act," or "You can't trust what they say."

- *Jezebel is without pity or compassion.* Jezebel goes after what she wants mercilessly: "Stone him that he may die!" This is a matter of her religion, Baal worship, versus the faith of Naboth. Deviance from her declared religious norm can't be tolerated. Ever notice how the most apparently "spiritual" people can be the most unkind, legalistic, and uncivil?

- *Jezebel wants total control and nothing less.* She could have taken the vineyard without killing Naboth, but this demon takes no chances, takes no prisoners. All opposition must be eradicated. When you encounter intransigence in religious affairs, unyielding inflexibility, beware—Jezebel's fingerprints may be all over your opposition.

- *Jezebel's purposes are aided by compliancy.* Jezebel understands only the language of authority and power. A sad commentary on the religious complicity of Israel's leaders is found in the words, "So the elders and nobles who lived in Naboth's city did as Jezebel directed in the letters she had written them" (1 Kings 21:11, NIV). She has just told them to lie, commit blasphemy, condemn an innocent man to death, subordinate their deeds to "scoundrels," and they conciliate without objection. In the Church, in the home, and in culture, going along with a definable agenda of the Jezebel spirit invites the worst possible outcome. Cooperation in any way is seen as weakness and invites further aggression by this demon.

LESSONS LEARNED FROM THE MURDER OF NABOTH

What happens next is instructive. The political and social leaders of Israel comply. No questions asked. There is a fast, some kind of gathering to follow, and Naboth is prominently seated. The lying villains come forward with their contrived accusations. The response is immediate. Naboth is murdered. All according to plan:

> *And two men, scoundrels, came in and sat before him; and the scoundrels witnessed against him, against Naboth, in the presence of the people, saying, "Naboth has blasphemed God and the king!" Then they took him outside the city and stoned him with stones, so that he died. Then they sent to Jezebel, saying, "Naboth has been stoned and is dead"* (1 Kings 21:13–14).

Not one person had the fortitude to challenge Jezebel. Here is another of her MO's. This demon counts on obliterating all opposition before it has a chance to band together. Jezebel's connivery is so effective that any individuated resistance seems hopeless. But if just one elder or noble had questioned this fatal scenario, the outcome might have been different. When Jezebel's purposes become clear to those with prophetic insight, silence isn't an option. Jezebel is a bully and counts on her potential adversaries wilting before the battle.

To further intimidate, Bible commentators also believe that Naboth's sons were also put to death along with him. That would have been the custom of the times; the guilt of a parent necessitated the punishment of his children. Once again we see that Jezebel eradicates all that is in her path. When you see Jezebel coming your way, you've only two choices. Get out of the way, which is spiritually unacceptable, or prepare to stand your ground and do battle. Know this: If you choose to compromise, Jezebel won't stop until she has destroyed all that you have and hold dear.

First Kings 12:16 summarizes the conclusion of the matter: "So it was, when Ahab heard that Naboth was dead, that Ahab got up and went down to take possession of the vineyard of Naboth the Jezreelite." Such was his right as a sovereign. After all, Naboth was a traitor to the crown, and the crown could now take what had been rightfully forfeited by his capital punishment. Jezebel wins. She shows Ahab who is boss by doing what he was apparently incapable of doing, despite his own wickedness. The spoils of war belong now to Jezebel.

The Bible doesn't tell us what happened in the aftermath of this seeming victory, but I can imagine there was a lot of rejoicing in the king's household. The king had gotten what he wanted. No matter that there was blood on his hands, and that Jezebel had taken another step forward in the consolidation of her power. Here is an insight into the spirit of Ahab, the complimentary demon to Jezebel. These two are a power couple from hell. Each abets the other. Almost always, where Jezebel is at work, the demon Ahab isn't far behind. Ahab lurks in the shadows as an accomplice to Jezebel's crimes. For example, suppose that the spirit of Jezebel sows discord in a religious enterprise. Look for an Ahab "yes-man (or woman)" nearby, clucking in agreement with all that Jezebel says and does. Ahab is Jezebel's cheerleader, or perhaps her unseen enforcer.

The tale seems to end here. But in the words of the late Paul Harvey, "Now, the rest of the story." Jezebel thought her evil plot was successful and all resistance had been swept away. Almost. But she hadn't counted on her old nemesis Elijah the Tishbite. Thank God for the Elijahs among us who won't bow to Jezebel! A prophecy is coming that will shake even the confidence of one as steel-spined as Jezebel. Judgment is about to fall. Jezebel thought that this bold man of God had been vanquished when he became suicidally depressed after his victory over Jezebel at Mount Carmel (see 1 Kings 19), but *he's back!* And boy, does he have a message for Jezebel!

Chapter 4

THE LOWDOWN ON THE SHOWDOWN

I'VE BEEN THERE. IT'S NOT REALLY A MOUNTAIN. CERTAINLY NOT what I, as an almost-lifelong resident of Colorado, think of a mountain. It's just a high hill, one of several in that part of Palestine. It was actually a series of connected promontories near present-day Acre, Israel. Jutting above land belonging to the tribe of Asher, it rose a little less than 2,000 feet above sea level, not exactly a formidable summit. But Mount Carmel is memorable for the showdown between the defiant prophet Elijah and Jezebel with her 850 prophets of Baal.

Jezebel, as you will recall, had imported from Phoenicia 850 pagan prophets of the demon god Baal when she married Ahab. In her quest to eradicate the worship of Yahweh, she had persecuted and killed the prophets of Israel. During this time, a man named Obadiah (his name means "servant of Yahweh"), who had administrative charge over Ahab's household, helped to hide 100 Jewish prophets in a limestone cave and kept them nourished there.

The Bible is silent about the exact nature of Jezebel's persecution, but we may be certain that it was cruel and bloody. She had succeeded in getting the general population to abandon the temple in Jerusalem. Whatever faithful prophets were left were marginalized as being "old school" advocates of an outdated religion. It's also probable that the drought Israel experienced at that time was blamed on the Jewish prophets. That too is typical of Jezebel. She's always blaming someone else for the problems she creates.

Interestingly, the confrontation on Carmel was precipitated by Ahab, not Jezebel. Ahab encountered Elijah and immediately accused the prophet of having something to do with the terrible drought that the country was suffering. This charge of wrongdoing on Elijah's behalf seems ludicrous on the surface, as if the prophet controlled the weather and for unknown reasons would want to bring suffering on Israel. Elijah didn't flinch. His answer was immediate and direct: "I have not troubled Israel, but you and your father's house have, in that you have forsaken the commandments of the Lord and have followed the Baals" (1 Kings 18:18).

In so many words, Elijah pointed back at Ahab to say, "It's your evil that brought this on." His turning of the imputation of guilt back on the king also included Jezebel, though her name isn't used here. We now glimpse something of the character of Elijah that Jezebel so feared. He offered no apologies to please King Ahab, as some weaker spiritual leader might have done. In reality he was being accused of a traitorous crime, punishable by death. But there was no plea for pardon and no admission of guilt from Elijah. His life was in Ahab's hands, but he didn't compromise. Essentially, he retorted, "It's all *your* fault, Jezebel included."

At this point, even the most bold of religious figures might have walked away, having made their point. No sense in pushing things and further ticking off Ahab and Jezebel. But Elijah wasn't finished. He was on a mission that was about to go to another level. He not only put the blame for the drought directly on the king, but he also made a bold challenge: "Now therefore, send and gather all Israel to me on Mount Carmel, the four hundred and fifty prophets of Baal, and the four hundred prophets of Asherah, who eat at Jezebel's table" (1 Kings 18:19).

FACING DOWN THE JEZEBEL SPIRIT

This is one tough dude! Previous to this Ahab had been searching for him, most likely to end his life. He had been living secretly in exile. Now he not only refused to take blame for the drought, but proceeded to demand an encounter with Jezebel's entire religious system! And what a system. Israel wasn't that populous at the time, so to have 850 pagan priests on the payroll, at government expense, was a big deal. In perspective, imagine the U.S. government bankrolling nearly 200,000 pastors and priests at taxpayers' expense?

Elijah was about to take on the Baals—plural. Not just one demon, but the whole religious hierarchy that Jezebel employed, which likely included entities such as Baal-shamin, Baal-zebub (from which we get the more commonly known Beelzebub), and Baal-Hamman. And the O.K. Corral was to be the summit of Mount Carmel.

That choice was first practical. It was wooded, and there would be plenty of kindling for fire. Second, this was the prior location for an ancient altar of the Lord (see 1 Kings 18:30) that had long ago been abandoned, "broken down." Plus, from this vantage point Jezebel couldn't miss seeing what was about to happen. Elijah was setting the stage for a clash between good and evil that wouldn't take place off the beaten path. It would happen where there could be no question about the outcome. This is the way to handle Jezebel. Get in her face. She only understands the language of spiritual confrontation. She counts on her adversaries running in fear of her intimidation and lies. Challenge Jezebel out in the open. Let everyone see her defeat and make note of what happens when her schemes are defied!

There were two categories of Baal's demon worshipers: (1) the prophets of Baal, and (2) the prophets of Asherah. (In reality, Asherah was the consort of Baal so they were quite literally, as we say, "in bed together.")

The distinction isn't clear, but we can make reasonable assumptions. The first group more likely represented the institutional religion of Baal, the administrators, teachers, and ritualistic leaders. The second group probably included the fortune-tellers, prognosticators, and oracles who provided the supernatural element of worship. The latter group was of Asherah, also known as Astarte of the Canaanites (a sexual, fertility goddess) and Ishtar of the Assyrians.

As already mentioned, these demon deities were just slightly different modalities of the same evil identity, Lilith, later to be known as Jezebel. Astarte, designated by the Greeks as Aphrodite, was depicted as naked, often with multiple breasts indicating fecundity. Debaucherous ceremonies were performed on her behalf. Ishtar, also a goddess of sex and fertility, was known for treating her lovers cruelly. Her trademark was "sacred" prostitution.

There is another possible distinction between the two groups of false prophets. It may be that Ahab and his retinue worshiped Baal and those whose royal favor was more inclined toward Jezebel focused on the goddess aspect. Jezebel's clairvoyantly-disposed prophets had a high place of honor, eating at her table as part of her household. They were like chaplains to her, personal advisors, like todays assorted cult gurus.

In whatever way the Baal gods were organized, Elijah would have been well familiar with these hideous idolatrous beings and the licentiousness surrounding their worship. He was undoubtedly incensed that a queen of Israel could sit on the throne and financially underwrite, with her royal treasury, such reprehensible indulgences. It had gone on too long, and now everyone would find out who was the true God as opposed to the satanic pretenders promoted by Jezebel.

But here is what's interesting. Ahab didn't question the challenge of Elijah. Whether it was misguided hubris or innate respect for the authority with which Elijah spoke, the King demanded that all the children of Israel gather with the prophets of Baal on Mount Carmel. There is no record that Jezebel put up a fuss. She apparently complied. Perhaps she was anxious to show up this interloper Elijah once and for all. It might even be surmised that she was so spiritually deluded that she thought her priests could win any contest. She didn't yet know what the challenge would be, but she was ready for it.

Many times when I am doing exorcisms I spot the manifestation of a Jezebel demon even before it speaks or gives its name. I know that look anywhere: the haughty arrogance and threatening defiance. There is a trademark demeanor of a Jezebel spirit that overstates confidence and defiance. Jezebel is consumed by her own exaggerated sense of superiority and overbearing pride. I'm certainly not the first exorcist to cast out a Jezebel demon, and other deliverance ministers have seen the same reaction from this evil spirit. Jezebel knows of past defeats but seems immune to her own history of failures. And no failure of Jezebel is more humiliating than what happened on Carmel.

First Kings 18:21 contains a challenge from the prophet of the Lord. I like how the classic King James phrases it: "How long halt ye between two opinions?" There was no grey area to Elijah. It was black and white, a clear choice. I like the verb from the NIV Bible—"waver" ("How long will you waver?") The NKJV says "how long will you falter?" This verse demonstrations inherently how to defeat the Jezebel spirit when it tries to work in stealth in your church or sphere of influence. Make it plain that a choice has to be made to serve God or Jezebel.

Jezebel will not be allowed to have her way. There will be no concessions; no reciprocal considerations: "If the Lord is God, follow Him; but if Baal, follow him," says Elijah. In modern language we might say, "You believe that Jezebel is right, than do what she says. If not, cast her out and follow the Lord with your whole heart. Either be controlled and manipulated by the Jezebel spirit, or be submitted fully to Christ and Him alone!"

Notice the response of Israel. Silence. Here is another practical lesson. If you confront Jezebel, don't expect those watching to come over to your side quickly with a hearty "Amen!" Jezebel is so crafty that her deception takes time, and spiritual power, to expose and defeat. Doubtless the disobedient Jews in Elijah's time were trying to figure out how to have it both ways—Yahweh and Baal. That's the spiritual and culture war of our generation. Many, even some Christians, want societal peace at all cost. They want the spiritual benefits of a biblically-based body politic, but also want to embrace what's politically correct.

In the case of Jezebel's kingdom, they probably liked the sensuous, erotic culture she had introduced. Some of them consorted with temple prostitutes and justified it in the name of religion. I'm reminded of a religious leader I once confronted about his blatant adultery. He responded that God had given him special revelation that he could have two wives. He wanted the advantages of a life of peace and purpose serving Christ, but he was also seeking a way to satisfy his immoral impulses. That has Jezebel written all over it!

"I alone am left a prophet of the Lord, but Baal's prophets are four hundred and fifty men." That sentiment of First Kings 18:22 sums up how we all feel at times, alone, as if we are the only ones doing the right thing for Jesus. On most occasions our self-pity is slightly overblown; but Elijah's was accurate. Jezebel had decimated the rest of God's true prophets, forcing the ones who escaped death to hide in caves and keep silent. Attempt to face down the Jezebel spirit and you may find yourself standing alone. Been there, done that. The timidity of others is a combination of fear and compromise; fear of what wrath any opposition to Jezebel will incur, and compromise that assumes things can be both God's way and Jezebel's way.

TIME FOR THE SHOWDOWN

So, here stands this lonely man on a mountaintop facing the entrenched religious empire of Jezebel. Showdown time. High noon on the Carmel main street. There are no lofty speeches. Elijah doesn't even try to persuade the people of Israel of their errors. When facing Jezebel, the time for talking is over. No persuasive argument will win. It's all-out spiritual war.

Jezebel loves to trap her victims with reasoning such as, "No sense in being a fanatic," or "This will all blow over in time," or "I'm sure we can bring both sides together on something we can agree upon." Jezebel has to be confronted, rebuked, her intentions laid bare, and given no reprieve.

Elijah's instructions are straightforward. Bring two young bulls. Let the prophets of Baal choose which one they want and cut it in pieces as an offering to their god. Lay it on an altar to be fueled by wood; but no striking of a spark to start a flame. Then Elijah will do the same. The devotees of Baal will pray to their god and Elijah will pray to the Lord. Then what? "The god who answers by fire he is God." When you realize a Jezebel spirit is at work it's fair to ask for a "trial by fire." Put whatever matter Jezebel is messing with to a test to see what is truly of the Lord.

I can tell you what often comes next: the accusation that you are "judging." Today's Jezebel will throw Matthew 7:1 at you ("Judge not, that you be not judged"). Remember, this is one of the most misapplied Bible verses. Matthew didn't mean that any one, especially a Christian, gets a free ride for any kind of bad behavior. The warning of this Scripture is that the person judging will be judged by the same standard by which he judges. The emphasis is *not* on avoiding all judging, but to not judge hypocritically and with malicious intent. Spiritual fruit can and should be judged. Judgment that comes from legalism is destructive; judgment to rein in immorality can be appropriate and necessary. Jezebel isn't interested in bad judgment, she wants *no* judgment. No curtailing of her agenda. No restricting her deviousness. No judging!

Elijah is so certain that God is on his side that he gives the prophets of Baal first crack at proving their stuff. And he does it with sarcasm: "Choose one bull for yourselves and prepare it first, for you are many" (1 Kings 18:25).

He gives the opposition every opportunity to misstep, plenty of rope to hang themselves. Sometimes when I'm doing an exorcism with Jezebel, I let the demon go on and on, as I did with Leanna in chapter one. Jezebel loves to hear herself talk and especially brag. The assured man or woman of God facing Jezebel need not be afraid that this demon's boasting is any threat. Pride always goes before a fall, and bragging often precedes miscalculations.

Now Jezebel and Ahab and all the prophets of Baal are ready. We can assume that Jezebel wouldn't have missed this for anything, though we aren't told she was present. She most certainly had spies reporting on this big event.

It's time for a trial by fire.

Let the games begin.

Chapter 5

THE GAMES ON CARMEL BEGIN

I CAN ONLY IMAGINE THE GLEE OF AHAB AND JEZEBEL AS THE CON-frontation on Carmel began. This lofty perch was believed to be the spiritual dwelling place of Baal. Thus the pagan prophets would have a distinct advantage. From Elijah's perspective, this had no consequence. Only the reality of the true God, who is omnipresent, was important. The key issue was that Israel could no more straddle the fence regarding which supernatural being would guide the nation. One deity was an impotent imposter and that was about to be revealed.

The odds weren't on the side of Elijah: 850 to 1! Every other prophet of Israel was hiding. He was alone against Jezebel. The followers of Baal believed that their god brought fire and lightning so they had momentum on their side. Plus they had told the general public that the drought was all the fault of the prophets of Israel, as pointed out in the last chapter. I can imagine that they were insolently anxious to prove their point, spurred on by Jezebel. I can imagine her sitting with them at their last supper as they prepared strategy, mocking Elijah over much wine.

Jezebel, blinded by her arrogance, really believed that her prophets were going to win.

The extraordinarily excessive, inordinate opinion that Jezebel had of herself blinded her to the fact that her prophets might actually lose. "You just can't do this to me," a demon of Jezebel once said to me. "I've had this bloodline for thousands of years. I've worked hard to destroy them. There is no way that you can get rid of me that easily. It's just not right that you should be able to cast me out when this woman needs me so much."

A similar conversation could have occurred as Jezebel's Baal prophets mocked the prophet of God. They had numbers on their side. They had public approval in their corner. And above all, Jezebel was their patron. She paid their bills. She was the most powerful person in the country. She even rolled her eyes in disgust at the timidity of her own husband Ahab when his name came up. There is no more self-assured attitude than that of the Jezebel spirit. She's a bully who will bluff you, if you're not careful. She believes her own press reports, what her demonic spin doctors say about her. "You are mighty Jezebel. No one could dare resist you."

NO SECOND FIDDLE FOR JEZEBEL

Jezebel shares her glory with none, including other demons. In many exorcisms I have observed Jezebel punish another lesser demon for daring to claim he was above Jezebel, or for failing to carry out Jezebel's instructions. Consider as an example a woman named Clarissa. She came to me suffering from severe physical pain that the doctors couldn't cure. In the course of our ministry time I discovered that she had many demons resulting from generational sins of violence and witchcraft. These were all linked to demons of infirmity, plaguing her with discomfort that no analgesic affected. Through inner healing work with her emotions we resolved Clarissa's own anger issues that caused her belligerent outbursts. Eventually, an evil spirit of Murder surfaced.

"I am the Strong Man," Murder bragged. "I'm the one her ancestors invited in when they killed and pillaged. They lived for war and conquest. And now I am the conqueror of this woman's life."

No sooner had the demon of Murder made that boast, than he suddenly cringed in fear. He contorted as if someone was beating him with intense force. He pleaded with this unseen, supernatural assailant to stop. "Who is tormenting you?" I demanded to know.

"Jezebel!" Murder screamed. "Make her stop."

"I not only won't make her stop, I demand that she intensify what she's doing to weaken you."

In minutes, the demon of Murder was enervated so much that he hardly opposed me. It was then that I called up the spirit of Jezebel to judgment. "He had no right to claim he was the most powerful," Jezebel said. "I am above every demon. None of them dares challenge me. I made Murder pay for claiming he controlled this woman. I do!"

I've learned from many years of experience that in the spirit world not many demons dare to exalt themselves above Jezebel. Generally, only demons with a Luciferian rank hold higher status. Some such as Baal and Moloch (the Canaanite god of infanticide) work in concert with Jezebel, but few try to trump her. This fact can be used during deliverance to "divide and conquer" by playing one demon off against the other.

Divide and conquer. That's what Elijah was doing. Divide the general population of Israel from the prophets of Baal by showing their paucity of power, and that would drive a wedge between the populace and Jezebel. Show up the religious leaders chosen by Jezebel, in order to expose false worship as being powerless, and Jezebel too would be stripped of all the power of her ascendency to the throne over Israel. Elijah was the man for the job and the moment of truth was about to arrive.

The prophets of Baal got things started. They took the bull they'd chosen and prepared it. Then they cried out to Baal, "Oh, Baal, hear us." Of course he couldn't; he wasn't there. A demon was the dynamic behind the worship, but demons need a body to work their evil. In this case, no priest could light the fire. It had to fall from heaven. So they yelled louder. Nothing. They didn't let up. They persisted from morning until noon, the passage of at least several hours. When that didn't work they "leaped" on the altar. This doesn't mean that they jumped on top of the bull. They doubtless were leaping around the altar in some kind of ecstatic, trance-inducing dance. Like whirling dervishes, they twirled frantically with abandon, and probably with considerable sensuality (since that was the nature of Baal worship).

It was all rather pathetic. I can only imagine what was going on in hell as Lilith scrambled for a strategy to overcome the obvious obstacle—no fire was falling. Wherever Jezebel was located at the time, her demons were likewise befuddled. I've often seen Jezebel in a state of agitation when things aren't going her way, especially when sins are confessed and curses have been broken and she is about to be cast to hell. Her previously confident demeanor resembles a panic, like rats scurrying to exit a sinking ship. I've heard Jezebel beg: "Just let me stay. I'll be good." (Yeah, right.) "Let me go into someone else who wants me." (No way.) "No, I'll go anywhere but to the Pit." (Come out in the Name of Jesus!)

Somewhere on Carmel or back in Jezreel, Jezebel may have paced the floor in frustration. Ahab might have cursed under his breath, damning the day he agreed to this contest. Nothing was going to work. Know this, that no matter how clever Jezebel's designs may be and how intricate her plots are constructed, with persistent prayer her purposes will come to an end.

Meanwhile, Elijah stepped up the pressure on Baal's prophets by mocking them: "Cry aloud, for he *is* a god; either he is meditating, or he is busy, or he is on a journey, or perhaps he is sleeping and must be awakened" (1 Kings 28:27). The Living Bible states what many commentators think Elijah was really sarcastically saying: "Perhaps he is... sitting on a toilet!"

Perhaps the irony served several purposes. We'd say he was egging them on. The more frantic they got, the sillier they looked and the more abject their failure would seem. Elijah likely wanted those watching to have no doubts that Baal's prophets had done their best job; no halfhearted effort. The sarcasm only made them more intense and pushed them to greater extremes. It worked. They screamed and cut themselves with knives, swords, and spears. I've seen similar ceremonies in the Far East in the name of various idolatrous deities. Up close and personal, sometimes inches away, I've seen pagans slice their tongues, push knives through their arms, legs, and cheeks. The demonic trance states required to accomplish these feats are induced by wild drumming and frenetic dancing, not dissimilar to what Elijah witnessed. The idea behind this self-torture is that by inflicting self-injurious punishment the gods are pleased. It was a way to appease Baal, short of human sacrifice.

The taunts of Elijah were also directed toward the pagan perception of Baal as an anthropomorphic god with human-like dimensions. Phoenician gods talked, fought with each other, drank to drunkenness, engaged in sexual misconduct, and, yes, even relieved themselves as humans do. He was demonstrating that the God of glory has no such physical limitations and can only be worshiped in spirit and truth (see John 4:24).

When every eccentric effort of Jezebel's prophets failed, they resorted to prophecy. In some kind of religious ecstasy they proclaimed what were supposed to be messages of divine inspiration. Their words were probably endorsements of Baal's significance, which only made the contradiction more apparent. This frantic activity of Baal's prophets continued unabated for many more hours. Jezebel doesn't give up easily. And she still uses religion via prophecy to belie her failures. Things haven't changed much.

One way to spot Jezebel in modern Christianity is to look for ostentatious words of prophecy or predictions that are usually both terrifying and intimidating. Among non-Pentecostals these "words" from

God are less obvious and more subtly hidden in unsolicited advice and legalistic warnings designed to control. Among some charismatics these "words from the Lord" can range from the ridiculous to the dangerous. Jezebel in this disguise is hard to identify since she operates alongside genuine spiritual gifts. What I've said is not to disparage godly advice or legitimate revelations from the Lord, but with Jezebel so operative in these times, an ample dose of wisdom and discernment is needed to sort through real and bogus prophecies.

Having spent themselves during many hours of frenzied activity, the prophets of Baal were exhausted with nothing to show for their ardor. Now Elijah was ready for action. He approached the old, abandoned altar to Yahweh that was in disrepair. He methodically rebuilt it and encompassed it with a trench about three feet wide. The wood was arranged for a fire and the bull was cut and laid on the wood. Then Elijah instructed those assisting to fill the trench with water. And that wasn't enough. He had water poured on the bull being sacrificially offered and also poured water on the wood. A second time he had the bull and wood drenched in water. Then a third time. So much water was put on the altar that it ran over and filled the trench.

This whole drama was doubtless played out over some time to prove a point; the neglected God of Israel was capable of igniting the sacrifice with fire in spite of every attempt to prevent it. In my mind's eye I can see Jezebel and Ahab flinching with each pot of water, their guts getting tighter and tighter as Elijah literally "poured it on." My guess is that neither of these monarchs remotely imagined that their priests would fail and that Elijah would succeed. The tension inside Jezebel was rising moment by moment, with an emotional crescendo that was explosive. Beware, Jezebel doesn't take defeat well. The minister of God who chooses to take on this demonic force should be aware of the kickback that's coming.

Elijah stepped forward near to the water-soaked sacrifice and majestically called upon the Lord. He wanted more than fire. He wanted a demonstration of God's power that proved to Jezebel she had been defeated. "Let it be known this day that You are God in Israel!" (1 Kings 18:36). The fire fell! It consumed the bull offering and the wood; it incinerated the stones and even turned the water to vapor. It was no flash of lightning that some might attribute to atmospheric events. It was an all-consuming fire like that of the burning bush seen by Moses. It burned and burned until its purpose was accomplished.

"Now what are you going to do, Jezebel?" one might ask in retrospect. Elijah is a hard act to follow. To make matters worse, all the people (except the prophets of Baal, Jezebel, and Ahab) prostrated themselves and worshiped Yahweh, declaring, "The Lord, He is God!" (1 Kings 18:39).

AFTER THE FIRE, JUDGMENT

Don't expect Elijah to be magnanimous in victory. This was no ordinary conflict. The very essence of Jezebel and Baal worship had to be eradicated without mercy. What does this mean to us today? Obviously, we live in New Testament times under grace. And for those who know what comes next, defeating Jezebel is not a pretext to make heads roll; however, there is much to be learned by the slaughter of Baal's prophets. "Do not let one of them escape," Elijah demanded. So, First Kings 18:40 tells us that the false religious leaders were taken to the Brook Kishon and executed.

Here is what we can take away from this demonstration of judgment. When Jezebel is exposed, it is required of the people of God that they demonstrate their determination to cut themselves off completely from this spirit. Suppose that Jezebel has been discovered operating in the church. Excommunication is in order. If influencing a marriage, spiritual intervention by godly counselors and deliverance ministers is necessary. In this historic case, Elijah was enforcing the Law of Moses when Ahab would not. Lest anyone think that this mass killing was too harsh, remember what evil these prophets had done, encouraging every sort of perversion and immorality in the name of religion. With Jezebel's help they had succeeded in turning an entire nation away from

God and damning their souls. Israel was, after all, a theocracy; Elijah's judgment was the judgment of God.

As the reader will learn later in this book, the spirit of Jezebel is the font of the most despicable evils, including pederasty, bestiality, rape, and molestation. Whenever I learn that someone is a victim of such terrible wrongs I know that the demon of Jezebel can't be far away. In fact, I would estimate, based on the experience of nearly four decades of counseling ministry and upwards of 30,000 cases of documented exorcisms, that the demon Jezebel influences 90 percent or more of sexual abuse crimes. When a woman, or man, tells me they have been molested, I always look for the demon Jezebel hiding somewhere, in a curse or in the person seeking help. The execution of Jezebel's prophets is a model of how to deal with this spirit, even under grace, with determination, righteousness, resolve, torment, and speedy deliverance for those she holds captive.

But what happens next is a bit of a surprise!

Chapter 6

JEZEBEL'S EMPIRE
STRIKES BACK

A VICTORY IN BATTLE DOES NOT ALWAYS ENSURE CONQUEST IN WAR. Those who fight for earthly kingdoms soon learn that truth, or they face the possibility of future discouragement and defeat. A successful commanding officer in war knows that what really matters is the ultimate outcome of conflict. Spiritual warriors have no choice but to learn the most effective strategies in battle. There is no better example in Scripture and literature than what happened to Elijah after he defeated the prophets of Baal on Mount Carmel. He underestimated the resiliency and the determination of Jezebel. Those who minister deliverance can't afford to make the same mistake.

Fire had fallen from Heaven. The prophets of Baal had been slain. The battle for spiritual supremacy in Israel was over. Yahweh was declared supreme. Case closed—or so Elijah thought. In my decades of doing deliverance, I have learned that each battle with Jezebel is not over until it is *really* over. After Israel's long drought, suddenly there was "an abundance of rain."

For a brief time, Ahab and Elijah had a truce. Who knows what was going on in Ahab's mind? He might have momentarily seen the error of his ways. He retired to eat and drink, relaxing after the tense conflict on Mount Carmel. The Bible does not tell us what Jezebel was doing; but, if you knew Jezebel the way I know Jezebel, you'd be certain that grass was not growing under her feet. Her prophets may have been slain, and her religious kingdom humiliated, but Jezebel was still Jezebel. In all my years of ministering deliverance, I've never met a demon so tenacious.

Demons leave in different ways. Some cry, some sigh, some cough, some growl; but almost always Jezebel screams—*loudly.* She thrashes. Convulses. Restraint is often necessary. Physical violence is commonplace. Jezebel doesn't go down without a fight. I know this from experience. Elijah had no one to warn him.

AFTER VICTORY AN ABUNDANCE OF RAIN

Ahab was having dinner. Elijah was back on Mount Carmel, on his face before God, pleading with the Lord to send rain to Israel. Seven times Elijah asked his servant to gaze upon the horizon for any sign that weather conditions were changing. Six times the servant returned with a negative report. The seventh time Elijah's servant reported seeing a small cloud which was barely visible. It was enough. When God is at work, small things can become mighty by His grace. That barely discernible white puff of a cloud in the distance was the sign that Elijah was seeking. By faith he knew a mighty outpouring of rain was on the way, something Israel had not seen in three years.

Elijah was a man of great faith. He could take on odds of 850 to 1, and win. By faith he could see a potential deluge in a small white cloud. And yet, he could not perceive the danger that was lurking in Jezebel's palace. Was he oblivious to the possibility of her continuing treachery? In battle, a soldier learns to constantly look over his shoulder; yet, Elijah seemed unconcerned about a sneak attack from Jezebel.

Those who discern Jezebel's activities can't afford that oblivion. I've dealt with almost every kind of demon in Satan's kingdom. None has the cunning and treachery of Jezebel. I'm not just talking about strategy during an exorcism. Jezebel's insidiousness affects everyday life with equally threatening determination.

Pastors who have fallen prey to Jezebel didn't see her coming. The married woman who came for counseling seemed desperately sincere. How could he ever fall into her arms? The deacon who occasionally disagreed with how church affairs should be administrated didn't seem like the kind of man who would lead an insurrection to kick out the pastor. The young associate minister fresh out of Bible college and so filled with enthusiasm didn't appear to be the kind of person who would try to take over and destroy a 20-year pastoral tenure.

Jezebel never looks like Jezebel. That is why she is so successful. She is the evil spirit of a million faces, most of them looking harmless and donning the guise of approbation. She flatters. She connives. She ingratiates herself with spiritual gifts and comes with no strings attached—in the beginning. Perhaps Elijah's mistake was to be focused on ridding Israel of Baal and bringing life-giving moisture to a thirsty land. In ministry, in family, and in society, we sometimes focus on the urgent and neglect the important. If Jezebel encroaches on your territory, in the home or in the sanctuary, that matter demands immediate attention. Like Elijah, you may be focused on what you think are more important spiritual things. But never, ever, ever, turn your back on Jezebel.

The rains came just as Elijah said they would. So great was the downpour that Ahab fled hastily to Jezreel with his chariot and horses. Elijah had no such transportation, so he ran on foot. The Bible tells us the spirit of the Lord was so mightily upon Elijah that he outran Ahab and his horses (see 1 Kings 18:46). Think, for a moment, what this means. Elijah had defeated Baal on Mount Carmel. Then he supernaturally outruns Ahab's horses for at least 16 miles. But he is running into a decisive confrontation with Jezebel. He has been mightily used by God but, where is his discernment about what is to happen next?

WHAT WILL JEZEBEL DO?

According to the Bible, at least the parts that are recorded, Ahab was the one who told Jezebel what happened on Mount Carmel. While that fact may be technically true, I find it hard to believe she didn't know the outcome of that contest. She had too much at stake. It would have been incompetent on Jezebel's behalf to sit by idly awaiting word about the battle with Baal. Maybe she didn't completely know what happened until Ahab informed her; but remember the Bible is not a literal transcript about every fact and event in the telling of any anecdote. My suspicion is this: Jezebel had well-placed spies watching what went on. And Ahab's eyewitness account wasn't exactly a revelation to her.

Even presuming that Jezebel didn't know about what happened on Mount Carmel, it's curious that the writer of First Kings says nothing about her reaction, only her actions. Did she fume slowly or explode with indignation? If she didn't know, was she shocked? Assuming it was a surprise, how long did it take to get her wits about her and devise a plan of evil action? Assuming she knew in advance, had she already decided how to retaliate? Whichever assumption is correct, the Bible is unambiguous about Jezebel's course of action.

Once again, I speak from personal observation after many encounters with Jezebel spirits. My experience teaches me that Jezebel is resolute. She doesn't waffle. She knows what she wants, and she sets out to get it with steely determination.

She is also retaliatory; revenge is her M.O. Cross Jezebel and she will make you pay. To confront this evil spirit, you must be certain that you have on the full armor of God and are just as unflinching as she is. When dealing with the Jezebel spirit, I tell you honestly that I haven't always succeeded due to some victims' reluctance to prevail spiritually. Not everyone who learns that they have a Jezebel spirit is immediately willing to give up the "benefits" they think the demon gives them. Once this demon becomes entrenched it is difficult to dis-lodge, whether in a person, a church, a marriage, or any relationship that has become destructive.

Jezebel sprang into action. She sent a messenger with a death sentence to Elijah: "So let the gods do *to me,* and more also, if I do not make your life as the life of one of them by tomorrow about this time" (1 Kings 19:2). In plain terms she declares that she will kill Elijah within a day or the gods may slay her! Failing to do that, she pronounces a curse on her own head: Her fate will be worse than the slain prophets of Baal.

Even given the erratic nature of Jezebel this is strange behavior. There had been a clear outcome to the rivalry between Elijah and Baal's prophets. The populace sided with Elijah when they saw fire fall. The nation of Israel was ready to return to the worship of God and declare Elijah their spiritual spokesperson. Ahab was too afraid to act against the prophet.

Jezebel does nothing ad hoc; she carefully calibrates everything she does. Isn't it somewhat puzzling that didn't she send a soldier in secret to slay him? Why should she warn her archenemy? Was she reacting impulsively? Or was there some method in her murderous madness?

The Bible only tells us what Jezebel did and what she said, not what was on her mind. My take on this is admittedly speculative, but I base my conclusions on the ways which I have seen the Jezebel spirit operate. As cool and collected as Jezebel can be, as sinister and methodical as she can scheme, like all evil spirits, Jezebel has flaws. We see these weaknesses in action here. Under duress, the Jezebel spirit can become impulsive, vengeful to a fault, and her own worst enemy. She may brag unnecessarily, react out of spite too quickly, and spring into action without adequate forethought. Those who confront Jezebel can use this demon's weaknesses to spiritual advantage

In the case of Elijah, Jezebel did not take a course of action that was in her best interests. Historians tell us that at the end of the Third Reich, Hitler was his own worst enemy, making poor military decisions and refusing to listen to his field generals. Such is the nature of evil. Pride blinds, power corrupts, and insolence distorts. When confronted with a Jezebel spirit, the child of God who is patient and seeks the Lord's wisdom will prevail. No matter how brilliant a spiritual strategist Jezebel may be, she eventually blunders to her own destruction.

The curse that Jezebel spoke over her own head, she uttered in the "name of the gods." She still didn't get the message that her gods were no gods at all. The oath of the death curse she proclaimed did not acknowledge the supremacy of Yahweh which had been dramatically demonstrated on Mount Carmel. The power of God had defeated her religious system, but she wouldn't admit it. In spite of reality, she clung to a power base that no longer existed. All Israel had turned against her; yet she was blinded by her own evil.

The book of James tells us that the demons believe and "tremble" (see James 2:19). They know they have lost the war of the ages. Demons realize that John's Revelation speaks the truth. They are defeated; still, I've never seen a demon surrender voluntarily. No demon ever asks to be saved. They never request any measure of God's grace. Any fool could have told Jezebel it was all over, but she would not hear it. How different history might have been, how different our world might be today if Jezebel had repented.

Chapter 7

RUN, ELIJAH, RUN

IT IS AXIOMATIC TO ONE WHO MINISTERS DELIVERANCE: *NEVER RUN from Jezebel!* But we have the benefit of hindsight. Elijah did not. Even so, I find his actions strange. The moment he learned of the death threat uttered by Jezebel, the Bible says that he "arose and ran for his life, and went to Beersheba..." (1 Kings 19:3). There he left his servant and ran another full day's journey into the wilderness. He was taking no chances and was obviously determined to get as far from Jezebel as he could. Beersheba was about 95 miles from Jezreel, followed by his running further, into the wilderness. There he sat down under a tree and prayed for death: "It is enough! Now, Lord, take my life, for I am no better than my fathers" (1 Kings 19:4).

Things had not gone as Elijah anticipated. Perhaps he had expected the kingly court and the entire country to turn to God as a result of the miracle on Carmel. When that didn't happen he became depressed, clinically depressed! There was no 911 to call or Prozac to pop, so he ran in desperation. He fled alone so no one would know where he was, leaving behind his servant in Beersheba. His actions seem a bit cowardly, but we know that he didn't lack courage because he had demonstrated bravery in taking on Baal's prophets. What are we to make of this episode?

It's obvious that Elijah now had doubts about what he was doing. He was probably physically exhausted. The tide hadn't turned his way despite the victory he'd won. I can sympathize. In long battles of spiritual warfare with Jezebel and her evil hordes, I too have felt, in my natural instincts, like taking a break. The battle with demonic forces can make one weary, especially the unrelenting stubbornness of a Jezebel spirit. It wears on you. I can't say that I've ever wanted to die, but there are times I've wanted to call it a day and take an extended time-out. That's when the deliverance minister must reach down inside where the Holy Spirit dwells and call upon supernatural grace to go forward.

MY OWN EXPERIENCE WITH DEMONIC FATIGUE

As I write this chapter I'm reminded of a deliverance case just a few days ago that wore on me tediously. I could actually feel the oppression in the room so strongly that I struggled to stay awake. Several times I stood to walk around the room just to keep my blood flowing and force myself to keep from nodding off.

Meanwhile the demon jutted out the jaw of the victim in a sign of defiance. "I am so angry. You were never supposed to find me," she said. "I had this woman in the palm of my hand until you showed up. I'm going to go mute. I just won't talk."

Jezebel turned her head aside and folded her arms. "I molested this woman, and she doesn't even know it. She was so young. I did the same to her mother, and I'll do the same to her child. Now, I'm not going to talk anymore." And the demon didn't speak for some time.

I needed to know the root of the curse that led to the host's possession, and interrogating Jezebel was the only way to find out. But the demon was going to show me who was boss by not speaking. Add to that my sheer exhaustion, and you can understand why I might want to "run" like Elijah. But I've learned in the past that nothing does more to defeat the spirit of Jezebel than demonstrating an even greater defiance than that of the demon.

In this case, just mentioned, I paced the room, prayed incessantly, fought back my weariness, and prevailed by God's grace and power. The demon eventually revealed that a multi-generational curse of incest had empowered Jezebel's evil. Once that ancient wickedness was renounced, Jezebel's resistance was sufficiently weakened and the woman seeking help was delivered. It wasn't easy. Thank God there was no juniper tree for me to sit under as there was for Elijah. I had no shade and was forced to tough it out. With the Lord's strength, Jezebel was cast out.

I certainly can sympathize with Elijah. There he sat, alone and forlorn. He was tired from traveling, the sun was hot, he was hungry, and there was no shoulder to cry on. He was all alone in the desert bearing the crushing burden of facing a wicked woman who had issued an order that he was wanted, not "dead or alive," but *dead*. In this condition, he asked not for strength and courage but for death.

Not a single commentator that I've read who writes about this incident hits the mark about what was really happening. This was no ordinary state of discouragement. Elijah was under demonic attack by evil spirits of Despair, Suicide, Death, and Defeat. He was suffering from spiritual oppression to the max. And those demons had been sent directly his way by Jezebel. Run though he did, the demons knew where he was and they put in his mind the idea to end it all. Think, for a moment, how the spiritual legacy of all those who follow the anointing of deliverance might not be able to minister today if Elijah had died then and there? If he had caved in to Jezebel then, what would we do now?

I am not inclined to be too hard on Elijah, but the fact is that he believed a lie. "I am not better than my fathers," he stated in First Kings 19:4. That thought did not come from God or even his own discouragement. In fact, Elijah walked in the miraculous as much or more than any prophet before. And he could not yet understand the legacy that he would leave to Elisha who would roughly double his spiritual output. At that moment he saw himself as a loser. He lost spiritual perspective. Jezebel is famous for causing that.

Spiritual leaders assaulted by Jezebel may not remember the many times they have mightily ministered in the Name of Jesus. They fail to recall all the victories over sin and Satan. Their perspective becomes skewed by spiritual oppression, and they give in to the deception of evil by thinking all they've done for the Lord is for naught. Some deacon is making their life miserable. Some member of the congregation is causing a fuss and threatening to cause a church split. Some friend with whom they have walked in fellowship has turned away and now ignores them. They feel alone, isolated, and vulnerable. If you are ever in that condition, look out! Jezebel is waiting, like a roaring lion, to pounce on you.

Don't look for a juniper tree to crawl under. Don't sequester yourself in a corner licking your wounds. It really is true in spiritual warfare that when the "going gets tough, the tough get going!" Never forget that Jezebel is a bully and counts on your backing down without a fight. Witness Elijah. He was not even putting up a fight against that hag. The result was deeper and deeper depression, to the point of total despair.

ELIJAH NEEDS HELP

Elijah was in need of serious, divine intervention. You need the same when you encounter Jezebel. This is real spiritual warfare, not evangelical cliques, politically correct language, or theological pleasantries. Thank God that an angel is always waiting to smite the evil emissaries of Jezebel and offer you provisions. Elijah's angel even cooked him a meal (see 1 Kings 19:5) on a hot fire. Now that's first-class room service. But the prophet is so disoriented that he sees the jar of water and the cake baked on coals and rolls over and goes back to sleep. A second time the angel touches him and offers some practical advice: "Arise and eat because the journey is too great for you" (1 Kings 19:7).

True spiritual warfare against Jezebel is always pragmatic. The one who confronts Jezebel needs to know when that evil spirit has the upper hand and is operating from a position of strength. Don't take on Jezebel under those conditions. There are times I've been ministering healing and deliverance when Jezebel manifests, and I do nothing at the time. The host individual may have curses that need to be broken or issues that need healing. To take on Jezebel while she holds all the cards isn't wise. Backing off isn't retreat. It is wisdom, waiting for a better chance when proper counseling and prayer ministry have removed the demon's spiritual legal rights and emotional strongholds.

The angel didn't tell Elijah to get on with the fight against Jezebel. On the contrary, the directive was to replenish his strength with food and prepare to fight another day. The coming journey to Mount Horeb that Elijah was to embark upon would take him 40 days! Without God's supernatural provender, this might have been the end of the story and a final victory for Jezebel after Carmel's defeat.

Pause for a moment and think about what Elijah experienced from the hand of God: fire falling from Heaven and the absolute defeat of Jezebel's religious system in short order; a meal supernaturally prepared by an angel; sustenance that was able to sustain him for 40 days and nights! Surely by now this prophet has gotten the message that the Lord is mightily with him and Jezebel's plans are doomed to failure. But, no. He does not "get it." The reader will soon see that upon arrival in Horeb he plunged again into defeatist depression. More on that in a moment, but for now note the following.

ELIJAH'S EEYORE COMPLEX

It seems obvious to me that Elijah is suffering some serious spiritual oppression from Jezebel's demons. The man of God can't think straight. His spiritual radar is way off. He should be operating in confidence and surety but instead acts bipolar. This is a sure sign of demonic attack, when Jezebel turns up the heat and you become spiritually disoriented. Jezebel is one powerful demon, never to be underestimated.

Once he arrived at Horeb, one would imagine that Elijah would call for a victory celebration. Instead, he was still suffering from the Jezebel juniper-tree complex. Only this time, instead of a tree, he resorts to a cave. His condition is getting worse. Jezebel's spiritual pressure is so great that the prophet quite literally crawls in a hole in the ground! Seemingly amnesic, he can't remember his recent triumph and launches into a pity party (see 1 Kings 19:10): "Woe is me, I've been the good guy when Israel wanted nothing to do with God and turned to paganism. And now I'm the only one left that is faithful to God, and the thanks I get for my sterling spirituality is that they now want to kill me. Woe is me" (Larson's translation). It all sounds rather self-serving and pathetic, a bit like Eeyore the donkey, the pessimistic, gloomy friend of Winnie-the-Pooh, always crying, always whining.

"I alone am left." Does Elijah's lament sound too familiar? Have you said something similar when licking your wounds after Jezebel retaliated because you took a stand for the Lord? Satan wants you to feel like you're all alone, the only one doing what God needs done. Not only is that a bit egotistical, it's simply not true. In every age and every place the Lord has those who have been faithful to His Name. But Jezebel knows that if she can get you feeling self-important with a bit of a persecution complex, she's winning. As far as I know, there aren't many in ministry who have faced the spirit of Jezebel as many times as I have under as many different circumstances. But before making that sweeping assumption, I must admit that I don't have a divine perspective. There may well be unheralded, choice servants of God I've never heard of who have borne the brunt of battle with Lilith and her ilk more, whose spiritual experiences are similar to mine.

God's response to Elijah's lament was to get the prophet's attention with a violent windstorm, an earthquake, and a fire. (Read First Kings 19:11–12.) The lesson was that God's presence was not in these dramatic displays of the elements. Instead the Lord came to Elijah in a "still, small voice." What a rebuke to this mercurial, bombastic prophet! And if this great man of God had a lot to learn about how to handle Jezebel, perhaps a good dose of humility is due for all those who engage the forces of darkness. I've heard preachers and pastors brag about taking on Jezebel and boast of their exploits. I cringe slightly at such bragging rights. No evil spirit is more cunning and adept at spiritual deception. Beware any vaunting over victories concerning Jezebel lest the boast become a vainglorious prelude to serious spiritual setbacks.

Before leaving this rendition of Elijah's emotional dysfunction, note that he still strives with the Lord over his predicament. Yet another supernatural occurrence takes place. God actually speaks to the prophet and asks him, "What are you doing here hiding in this cave?"

The question is, of course, rhetorical. The Lord is omniscient and knows exactly what is going on, but the inquiry brings out yet another depressed expression of regret and even more self-justifying pretentiousness: "I have been very zealous for the Lord God of hosts; because the children of Israel have forsaken Your covenant, torn down Your altars, and killed Your prophets with the sword. I alone am left; and they seek to take my life" (1 Kings 19:14).

Perhaps, like me, you're tempted to roll your eyes and utter, "C'mon, Elijah, give us a break with all this self-deprecation." We can only imagine that this didn't go over too well with Jehovah. Elijah had already made this point four verses earlier, and it's as if he is oblivious to the fact that the Lord has previously heard this outworn argument. It all speaks to me of the lack of emotional direction the prophet is experiencing. Is he being a bit psychologically self-indulgent? Yes, but remember who he is up against. Lest we be too hard on Elijah, let this sad chapter of his life serve as a warning to those who engage Jezebel on the field of spiritual combat. If you intend to take on this demonic personification of unadulterated evil, be prepared, prayed up, and as full of God's Spirit as you can be. Jezebel is one tough cookie and before you eat her alive, she may have you for lunch!

Chapter 8

TIME OUT FROM
FIGHTING JEZEBEL

AFTER THE VICTORY ON MOUNT CARMEL AND EVEN AFTER ELIJAH runs from Jezebel in fear, God is not finished with Elijah. Those who know the story understand there are some great chapters left in his life. But for the time being, it doesn't look good. Jezebel has made him a hunted man-on-the-run. Jezebel's defeat at Mount Carmel seems to have resulted in even more intransigence on her part. This relentlessness has left Elijah discouraged, depressed, wanting to die. God knows that this otherwise bold prophet needs a break, a time out. So the Lord sends him to the wilderness of Damascus to do what he can't in Israel right now: influence the future of a nation by anointing the new king of Syria.

Damascus is enough distance to be safe from Jezebel's immediate pursuit. Now Elijah will be instrumental in preparing for the transition that will occur when Jezebel's judgment arrives. God tells Elijah to also anoint Jehu to be king over Israel. Jehu was clearly a regent-in-waiting, as was David while Saul still reigned. God's inexorable wheels of justice regarding Jezebel are turning, and Jehu will play a significant role.

There are lessons to be learned here. Those who intently take on Jezebel need a break now and then. This demon is so relentless and persistent that practical considerations of rest and refreshment from battle, as well as some distance for breathing room (such as Elijah's commission from God to go to Syria), are often crucial. I know. Fighting Jezebel is down-and-dirty warfare. It requires stubbornness, persistence, and dedication. No man or woman of God, no matter how strong they are in the Lord, can continuously keep up the pace of battle against this evil spirit. Jezebel would love for those who oppose her to wear out or get worn out. I have found that in times of such spiritual warfare it's good to take a breather by focusing on some normal things.

I remember ministering to a woman deeply bound by a spirit of Jezebel whose life was exceedingly dysfunctional. No wonder. She came from an ancestry that was a veritable moral cesspool. She had been incested by both biological parents. To complicate matters more, Mom was in Eastern Star and Dad was a Shriner, adding occult curses of Freemasonry. Further spiritual investigation uncovered murder, witchcraft, and organized rape and pillage on behalf of her forbearers centuries ago. All this generational baggage led to her a morally erratic life of promiscuity, drug abuse, and emotional breakdowns. I was happy to help her with prayer and deliverance, but it was a heavy load to work with her consistently. By the time it was all over and she was freed, I and the team assisting me were exhausted emotionally and spiritually. I was ready for my Damascus, a country far enough away that the horrors of a life driven by Jezebel was out of my mind. If I expected to be able to help others and go back into such intense battles, I needed my time out.

For me, time out is often the normalcy of an enriching marriage and a close family. That's my refuge, a place where I can unwind and deal with real world stuff. Every man or woman of God needs such a place. Your Damascus could be a special geographical location that's a retreat, or friends with whom deep emotional bonds exist. It can also be, as it is with me, the love of a spouse and the joy of parenting. To any minster of deliverance who reads this, and who with any regularity faces down Jezebel and Co., find your place of time-out before you burn out.

ELIJAH LEARNS HE'S NOT ALONE

During this respite from the machinations of Jezebel, God gave to Elijah an important message with a crucial truth. This courageous man of God who had a bit of an "I'm the only one" complex learns from the Lord that he's not alone holding the fort.

Yahweh declares: "Yet I have reserved seven thousand in Israel, all whose knees have not bowed to Baal, and every mouth that has not kissed him" (1 Kings 19:18). While that actual number may have been rounded off a little and was perhaps a representational amount, considering the population of Israel at the time, it was a goodly percentage of those living in the Promised Land. Seven is a symbolic number in Scripture and it may have been God's way of saying that there was a substantial portion of the nation that was still faithful to God. Despite an apparent lack of public display of fidelity and regardless of Jezebel's best efforts to stamp out true religion, many were at least privately faithful.

The Bible uses a unique expression here which isn't readily apparent to the average Westerner who has never been around a pagan, idolatrous society. It's not that unusual for those who worship idols representing deities, such as gods of Hinduism or Buddhism, to clothe, offer food to, or even kiss the idols of the particular religion. This ancient act of veneration is used by God as an example of the way this 7,000 had remained faithful. Their lips have not touched these gods made by the hand of man.

Deliverance is a unique ministry. Ask anyone who has followed that calling. It's an anointing that is misunderstood, mischaracterized, and even vilified. I know that fact personally perhaps better than anyone. Any disciple of Christ who responds to that mission must be prepared for being ostracized and suffering harsh judgments. At times of persecution those of us whom the Lord has privileged to set the captives free must remember: *We are not alone!* Seven thousand, or 70 thousand, or maybe even 70 million have quietly, without fanfare, refused to bow before Baal. They have not kissed the feet of Satan nor succumbed to Jezebel's deception. There is a mighty army of warriors unafraid of Jezebel's threats and retaliation. There are many more opposing Jezebel than might be imagined.

What do you do while you're in your own Damascus? Rest. Recuperate. Reevaluate. Restore. Refortify. The war with Jezebel will resume soon enough, so take advantage of having some time off-duty, functioning as a spiritual "civilian" without immediate demands to have your guns loaded and ammunition battle ready.

REST FROM JEZEBEL

I'm not suggesting rest entails improving your golf score or being a couch potato. There are different kinds of rest. For me it's a rest not to be expending emotional and spiritual energy combating Jezebel directly. It's understood that spiritual warfare is never-ending and that the devil prowls constantly, seeking an opening into our lives (see 1 Pet. 5:8). But this isn't the same as nose-to-nose dealing with the devil. If you do it that way, and I don't know any other way, it's exhausting. Jezebel is wily, clever, and conniving.

Fighting this evil influence is a spiritual chess match with eternal checkmates. From a standpoint strictly of the physical and emotional outlay of energy, nothing is quite comparable to a demonic battle with Jezebel. You can't let down your guard for a moment. Strategically, you always have to be thinking several steps ahead. The soulish energy output is unlike anything one encounters in any other realm of life. Spiritual speaking, it's the World Series, World Cup, and Super Bowl wrapped into one.

Bottom line: If you minister deliverance, you will encounter Jezebel. And you will need to discover your own way of finding rest.

RECUPERATE FROM JEZEBEL

Spiritual warriors get wounded. They sometimes get shot. They all have battle scars of some sort. We've already discussed how Elijah's confrontation with Jezebel took an enormous toll on him. Who among us has ever literally called down fire from Heaven? Then, by spiritual comparison, we might not be any better than Elijah when it comes to handling the afterglow of spiritual victory. And if he suffered so severely following his fight with Jezebel, we too might need some recuperation time.

Jezebel is very good at inspiring timidity and even fear. She plants suggestions of retribution that may be hard to shrug off, especially if those intimations of revenge are directed at loved ones. I've lost track of the times that Jezebel threatened the most unspeakable retaliatory actions against my wife and children. I don't succumb to the fear such intentions are designed to instill. Not for a moment do I think that this demon will be successful in carrying out these kickbacks. God is more powerful!

My trust is in a God who promises, "A thousand may fall at your side, and ten thousand at your right hand; but it shall not come near to you" (Ps. 91:7). Many is the time I have thrown back into the teeth of Jezebel the promise of Isaiah 54:17: "No weapon formed against you shall prosper, and every tongue which rises against you in judgment You shall condemn. This is the heritage of the servants of the Lord."

Still, the constant need to thwart every attack with both defensive and offensive actions can take a toll on a human level. No matter how strong one's faith may be (once again, remember Elijah), sheer physical exhaustion can take a toll over time. It is okay to admit that reality and take time to recuperate so your soul can heal from the arrows of accusation aimed your way by Jezebel.

REEVALUATE WHAT YOU'VE LEARNED FROM JEZEBEL

Time out is time for reevaluating what you've learned in the latest battle. I've had thousands of confrontations with spirits of Jezebel—I'm talking about actual exorcisms, not just "prophetic" encounters that can be dismissed all too easily with quiet, calming prayers. I'm speaking of extremely physical, noisy, coughing/spitting and sometimes regurgitating conflicts with demons of Jezebel that kick, gouge, scream, assault, and even punch with superhuman abilities. In each exorcism I learn something new, usually a unique tactic of Jezebel I haven't experienced before. If I, as a well-seasoned veteran of such warfare, am still on a learning curve, the novice certainly needs to take time to ponder what he's been through.

If I consider just the Jezebel combat situations I've experienced in the last 30 days (as of the time I am drafting this book), here are some unique lessons I have learned:

- A married woman living in an emotionally or physically abusive relationship can give Jezebel a legal right to operate in her life by submitting to her spouse's illegitimate authority. Most pastors advising such a woman would quote First Corinthians 7:14 to insist the woman remain actively involved in the marriage to save ("sanctify") her husband. But Jezebel can use such a situation as a means to torment the wife, who should remove herself (perhaps by a temporary separation) from this spiritually unlawful soul bond.

  Lesson learned: *Christian counseling which follows "standard procedures" may in fact, without realizing it, deliberately put a woman/wife at risk of demonic bondage.*

- A male can have a spirit of Jezebel from an incestuous relationship with his mother. The individual who represented this principle had a mother who herself was incested and raped. In her bitterness she cursed her own son, seeking to destroy his destiny out of jealousy that he might have a life better than she had. This pathological way of thinking may seem contrary to all we surmise about motherly instincts, but when Jezebel twists the mind, almost any depravity is possible.

Lesson learned: *Jezebel has no sexual distinction in terms of inhabitation and may display sociopathic behavior in those she possesses.*

- A woman who was on her fifth marriage, this time to a man struggling with porn, refused to see herself as any part of the problem. She thought her husband had a Jezebel spirit because of his lust. In fact, this woman was the Jezebel lightning rod for much of the evil surrounding her. When I challenged her assumption that she was the victim and not the perpetrator of evil in her home, she turned on me and read me the riot act. She tried to explain in detail why I was doing deliverance all wrong and was deceived by the devil. (Never mind my four decades of ministerial experience.) She saw her mission as setting my theology and methodology straight.

Lesson learned: *When Jezebel is confronted she may try to flip things to shoot the messenger and deflect fault to the one who is attempting to undo Jezebel's damage.*

- A middle-aged woman, involved in ministry, single for more than ten years, had vowed never to let another man into her life. After the divorce of her parents, her father had remarried the stereotypical evil step-mother. Desperate for some emotional connection, she allowed her stepbrothers to molest her throughout her teen years until she married at age 16. That union was short-lived, after which she swore that, since all men are obviously evil, no male would ever touch her again. Attractive, bright, spiritually astute, and with excellent social bearing, she would have had no problem finding a Christian mate. Instead, she lived in isolation aloof from all companionship. The exorcism uncovered a

20-generation curse on her mother's side that put her at risk to be abused by men.

Lesson learned: *The demonic scheme was to keep this lovely Christian woman from her destiny by encouraging her to believe that she'd be more effective for God with men out of her life; thus she was robbed of opposite-sex fellowship which stunted her ability to understand a broader scope of human behavior and be more effective in ministry.*

I could give many other examples of lessons I have learned during times of reevaluation. There will always be plenty of demons to go around and plenty of people in need to keep anyone in ministry busy 24/7, if that's the goal. But sitting back to reconsider what has been discovered along the journey can be a valuable guide to the next encounter with evil.

RESTORE WHAT JEZEBEL HAS STOLEN

Not only is the victim of Jezebel's attacks in need of spiritual restoration, but so is the one who ministers to that victim. Jezebel may have stolen your time, energy, ability to help others, sense of spiritual fairness, even your faith in basic human decency. The ordeal of battling demonic forces like Jezebel sometimes afflicts the one doing ministry with a degree of cynicism, even jadedness. Be careful to receive personal spiritual restoration. That can come with prayer, reflective meditation, wise counsel from others, even personal deliverance from bondages revealed by what you have encountered as you ministered to others.

It's common for Jezebel to attempt getting even by harassing the one who has defeated her. This is a vengeful, pernicious demon. She carries grudges, especially when she's been spiritually humiliated. Following her defeat by Elijah, Jezebel would have been smarter to lay low for a while, regroup and strike back more subtly; but, no, that's not how Jezebel operates. Don't be paranoid or fearful, but be on guard. The one attacking Jezebel will often bear the brunt of daring to defy this witch. So, being strong in the Lord and the power of His might is more important than ever. After confronting Jezebel, assess the toll on your own walk with the Lord and receive restoration before fighting again.

RECOUP THE DAMAGE JEZEBEL HAS DONE

Spiritual warfare takes a toll. The minister of Christ must take heed lest he fall through failing to recognize how Jezebel's deception has crept into his own life. Here are some tips based on the damage I've seen Jezebel do:

- *Refortify your theology.* Jezebel throws a lot of curve balls. Some are designed to question theological assumptions you've held. I've watched good men of God go off on dangerous, non-scriptural tangents after a Jezebel encounter. They adopt exotic doctrinal ideas that are not time-tested and contain the seeds of personal destruction. One pastor with whom I fellowshipped began to think that I wasn't deep enough spiritually, and that God had given him more revelation. He could minister quicker, better, and deeper. Then he arrogantly stated that his power and knowledge far exceeded my mentoring, even though my ministerial experience exceeded his by decades. Today, his ministry is marginalized and in serious decline.

- *Be accountable to older, wiser, and more experienced teachers.* I again draw this lesson from experience. A certain minister whom I taught and commissioned later developed some ideas about demons that simply weren't biblical. I called him on it, and he rebelled. The turning point was when he publicly, from the pulpit, began teaching what bordered on heresy. Others tried to talk to him, but to no avail. This man's following dwindled and he lost his church. Still he would not relent. I have to wonder if he too became tormented by the very Jezebel spirit he sought to vanquish.

If you want to be used of God for more than a few victories over evil, it takes pacing, timing, humility, and knowing when to retreat to your own Damascus. "It's you again," the demon Jezebel says to me time after time. "I get so sick of seeing you. Don't you ever give up?"

Not only is my tenacity important, but the reason I live to fight Jezebel another day is because I pace myself as best I can. I didn't always minister that way. When much younger in the faith I was far too tempestuous and impulsive. I rushed in where angels did, indeed, fear to tread. I'm not suggesting that I now have so much experience that I am beyond spiritual mistakes; but I have learned the lessons of this chapter the hard way. Please, benefit from my experience, and you too will someday earn the ultimate grudging accolade of Jezebel, "Not you, again."

Chapter 9

THE DEMON OF DEAD WOMEN

WHEN YOU'VE DONE AS MANY EXORCISMS AS I HAVE, IT'S DIFFICULT TO find one that really stands out. But there are few which, among the thousands I've been involved in, stand out as being extraordinarily unusual. Such was the case of a woman sentenced to jail for theft, stealing from a brothel. She was a prostitute, but wasn't sentenced for the crime of prostitution. It was unlawfully taking the proceeds of the whorehouse that put her behind bars. Some ladies with a prison ministry persuaded the warden to let the convicted felon come to one of my seminars.

As she received ministry there didn't seem to be much of an initial breakthrough, only the suggestion that her plight might have something do to with the idolatrous religion of Hinduism. That seemed strange, since this was a Caucasian woman in the Deep South. As I prayed with her the name Kali came to mind. You've already learned in chapter two that the Hindu goddess Kali is one of the many manifestations of Jezebel/Lilith. (The reader will recall that Kali is a highly sexualized, murderous manifestation of the Jezebel spirit.)

The moment I said, "Kali, if you're there, I command you come forward to face me," it was as if an emotional volcano had erupted inside this woman. I was reminded of the many times had I seen large idols of Kali in India. This demon is usually depicted coal black with large, bulging eyes, hovering over the body of a murdered lover, holding the head of her paramour in her hand. But how did Kali get from the Asian subcontinent to a humid and sultry city in the Bible Belt?

"Fifty generations," was the answer the demon gave. "I've been tormenting women in her bloodline for more than a thousand years!"

In deliverance ministry I rely on accumulated wisdom and the knowledge of Scripture as much as possible, knowing that moments of true prophetic insight aren't the norm. But in this case, the Lord granted me the revelation I needed. The word was, "suttee."

As I slowly and deliberately spoke the word, the demon screamed, "How did you know?"

Suttee (also called sati) is the ancient Hindu practice, now outlawed in India (but still practiced in some remote villages), of the widow of a dead Hindu man throwing herself on the burning funeral pyre of her deceased spouse, to be burned alive. Hinduism teaches reincarnation. Consequently, for the soul to be released from the "prison" of its physical encasement, the body must be cremated so the soul can thus transmigrate to its next life form. This form of immolation has been practiced by Hindus for more than 2,000 years and has been exported wherever Hinduism has taken root outside of India, especially in Bali where the most elaborate cremation ceremonies can be seen. I have witnessed these ceremonies where suttee was rumored to take place, though I did not see the actual immolation.

With the coming of the British Empire, and Christianity, to India in the 19th century, the practice of widow suicide was banished in 1829. At the time there were an estimated 500 to 600 such cases each year (at least those were the instances known to authorities). In one nine-year period following 1815, in just one state of India, British authorities recorded almost 6,000 cases of suttee. In Nepal, which is the only official Hindu kingdom on earth, suttee was legal until 1920. The practice was so revered that memorials were built to honor these women for their supposedly noble deed. In fact, women who did not burn themselves on the pyres were forced to suffer disgrace the rest of their lives. In some cases, where for certain reasons the deceased male Hindu was buried, the surviving wife was expected to be buried alive with the corpse. In some cases women were buried in sand and the Hindu priests danced on the grave, compacting the sand, until the woman was considered dead.

Occasionally a woman would try to escape, only to be forcibly held down in the flames. These factual accounts were published in the British press; they were not the fables of illiterate tribes. In some cases the pyre was placed in a pit, not above ground as I've seen it in India and Bali. This meant that the widow would be thrown into the hole, from which she could not escape if she wanted. In 1751, A Danish missionary to India wrote of witnessing 47 widows being burned at once.

Hindus do not represent the only belief system associated with wives sacrificing themselves upon the death of a husband. Ancient Thracians in the fifth century BC considered it an honor to have their throats slit on the grave of their deceased spouse. Historian Edward Gibbon notes that some Germanic tribes required a widow to hang herself over her husband's tomb. The Natchez tribe in the southern United States practiced the strangulation of widows upon a husband's death. Some Pacific island societies also used to demand the death of widows.

My purpose for this lengthy digression about this phenomenon is to link this aberrant practice to the spirit of Jezebel and degradation of women. Hindu women believed that by suttee they achieved automatic entrance into heaven, along with their husband. In an illiterate society, unreached by the gospel, this would be a powerful motive for suicidal sacrifice. In addition, some were told that this was the price to pay for the sin of being a bad wife. Obviously, the practice of suttee has Jezebel's fingerprints all over it. (And some contemporary critics of

Christianity have the nerve to claim that Christianity is the foremost religion that has suppressed women?)

Now that the reader understands the depth of what the Lord had revealed to me about this Bible Belt woman to whom I was ministering, it is apparent that only a word of knowledge from God could have unlocked the moral mystery of this woman's descent into prostitution and thievery.

What makes this encounter with Jezebel all the more unusual is that the Lord also showed me that her mind was embedded with the soul imprint of the actual woman who was associated with suttee. (Our ministry has released numerous teaching materials about this phenomenon that we call Ancestral Generational Dissociation, the fragmenting of consciousness from a past ancestor which is then genetically passed on through the bloodline.)

"I want to speak to the woman who committed suttee," I said with a bold step of faith. "What is your name?"

"Makesha."

"What happened to you, Makesha?"

"I was to be burned, but I tricked them. I wasn't going to die willingly. So, when the men came to throw me on the pyre, I seduced them. As I was having sex with them, I pulled out a knife and stabbed them to death."

As I have already described, that is what Kali does; she dispatches her lovers by beheading them. More than 1,000 years ago, Makesha's crime gave the spirit Kali (aka Jezebel) the right to carry on a curse, and now this 21st century southern belle was affected morally. Naturally there were other factors in this woman's troubled past, but the demons of Kali and Jezebel were behind the scenes, orchestrating as many circumstances as possible to reenact this ancient ritual of female self-destruction.

Procedurally, the exorcism of Makesha followed the protocol that the Lord has given me through many years of experience. The ancestral, fragmented soul part was made to realize the error of her murderous actions and was given the gospel to understand grace and forgiveness. Once that inherited memory identity received spiritual and psychological resolution, the curse of 50 generations was renounced and the spirits of Kali and Jezebel were cast out. But it is what the account teaches us about the demon Jezebel that deserves our immediate attention.

JEZEBEL IS ROOTED IN RELIGION

It should be no surprise that the curse of Makesha's bloodline came from a fanatical kind of Hinduism. How this evil strain got to the American South, we never uncovered. But all of us have distant ancestors who cross-pollinated sexually in many ways and across vast geographical areas. Perhaps her ancestor traveled through India to a Southeast Asian country or islands in the Pacific. Who knows? Somehow this demon became part of Makesha's genetic history and followed to wherever her ancestors migrated. Ancient Hinduism, with its caste system, history of child brides and women being treated as property, and demonic pantheon of gods, would have been an apt vehicle.

Jezebel is a religious spirit. No matter what evil is perpetrated, there is almost always a religious rationale. Spirituality may be twisted, such as an appeal to New Age ideas. It may be out-and-out paganism or witchcraft. Sometimes it veers into Satanism. When it takes on a semblance of Christianity, its veneer may be both both liturgical and Pentecostal, liberal and conservative. Since most readers of this book are likely to be evangelical or charismatic in theological persuasion, let's focus on how Jezebel works within that religious environment.

- *The prophetic:* Jezebel feeds on revelations and tries to control prophecies. Legitimate spiritual insights of the Holy Spirit are counterfeited as a means of dominating people and manipulating their behavior. My warning is this. When someone tells you that they "have a word from the Lord" for you, do some investigation before going off on a tangent to follow this "word." Ask hard questions. Find out who knows this "prophet" personally and can vouch for his personal life to determine whether he (or she) walks before the Lord in moral purity and theological consistency.

- *Healing:* Before you allow anyone to lay hands on you for healing prayer make certain that you have some accountable relationship with this person. It should be a pastor or evangelist that you know and in whom you have confidence. Be cautious of the latest-and-greatest healer who comes to town with a "miraculous anointing." Many times I've cast Jezebel demons out of people who were subjected to witchcraft by an itinerant "mighty man of God" without realizing it. Know who prays for you and whether they have a background in the occult. Even if they mean well, if they have no understanding of spiritual warfare, they may have lingering curses in their own lives which haven't been eradicated.

- *Extreme shepherding:* Beware the spiritual leader who tries to control the personal details of your life, such as who you have as friends and even a mate. When you hear a pastor say, "If you ever leave this church bad things will happen to you," that is the time to get out of that church—*fast!* You've just been cursed by a Jezebel spirit that will try to monitor the smallest details of your life. Good pastors give wise, loving counsel, but they never intrude in your personal affairs without their advice being sought. Even then, watch out if they attempt to manage your personal choices with a "thus saith the Lord" approach.

- *Regulating legalism:* If a spiritual advisor goes beyond personal convictions to tell you how to dress, act, even think— watch out. They may seem to have your best interests at heart, but their real agenda is to become firmly fixed in making you their personal alter ego. Later in the book we'll deal with something I call Dissociated Soul Transference, a kind of soul tie on steroids that allows the person with a Jezebel spirit to actually get inside your mind and influence your thoughts. Some think that Jezebel is all about lust and seduction, and that's definitely one modality of this evil spirit. But Jezebel may also swing the spiritual pendulum the other direction toward a self-righteous, works-centered kind of spirituality based on legalism. Don't allow your life to be regulated by rules and unbiblical demands that make you hostage to someone assuming illegitimate spiritual covering over your life.

JEZEBEL REEKS OF RELIGION

As we will learn in more detail, Jezebel is the spirit behind sexual perversion, sexual abuse, and all morally aberrant conduct. But Jezebel isn't always a seductress. Jezebel isn't necessarily found in sultry sexuality and décolletage. That's definitely one of her approaches, but Jezebel can also reek of religion and piety.

I recall dealing with one highly demonized woman whose own mother had molested her. The mother had gone to voodoo witch doctors to curse her own children. Yet those who casually knew this misguided mother at church thought of her as the ultimate example of a sweet, Christian woman. All her life mom had witnessed of Christ's saving grace. She prayed, read her Bible, and would be the first to register shock at cultural trends of immorality. Yet in her private life this morally inconsistent mother gossiped, cursed other Christians, and even sought out psychics. What are we to make of this hypocrisy? The duplicitous woman was likely mentally ill and perhaps suffered from dissociative behavior (multiple personalities) by which she was able to compartmentalize her different roles and views of spirituality. Above all, this mother was a Jezebel, and in fact the daughter was delivered

JEZEBEL

from the very same demons that her mother had handed down, generation to generation.

Jezebel isn't just religious, she's a fanatic. She the violent force behind radical jihadism. She's the demon driving some churches and whole denominations to adopt policies which directly conflict with Scripture. She walks the corridors of denominational headquarters, the classrooms of Bible colleges, and even sits in the pews of churches who make room for her.

My words shouldn't be construed as saying that every local church or organized Christian movement is led by Jezebel. There are many wonderful seminaries and Bible colleges where Jezebel couldn't get inside the door. There are dynamic churches that win souls and even minister deliverance where Jezebel hasn't gained a foothold. But at the same time we must not be so naïve to assume that just because something has a "Christian" label that Jezebel automatically stops at the front door. As we've already established, throughout the ages, Jezebel has clothed herself in the garments of religiosity. Where she can encourage actual immolation such as suttee, she will. But more often she will take on the demeanor of religion, "having a form of godliness" (2 Tim. 3:5) but denying its true power.

Chapter 10

OPENING THE DOOR
TO JEZEBEL

HOW DOES A PERSON GET A SPIRIT OF JEZEBEL? OBVIOUSLY, GENERA-
tional curses is one open door, as I have already covered. But even
ancient curses need something in this life with which to connect. In
my book *Curse Breaking: Freedom from the Bondage of Generational Sin*,
I establish a principle which needs to be reiterated here. I quote from
chapter 1 of that book:

> In spite of the inherent power of the words of a curse, the
> principle of cause and effect prevails. We learn this from the
> well-known proverb: "Like the sparrow in her wandering,
> like the swallow in her flying, so the causeless curse does not
> alight" (Prov. 26:2, AMP). The Living Bible puts it this way:
> "An undeserved curse has no effect." The intended victim of
> the curse will be no more harmed by an unmerited curse than
> by a bird flitting through the sky.
>
> This does not mean, as many Christians seem to think, that
> believers are immune to all curses. It means that the devil

can only activate curses based on true causes, and that maledictions cannot land on people just because their enemies hate them. Still, unfair as it may seem, some curse-causes are beyond our initial control because they occurred to our ancestors or to the members of a group to which we belong.

Satan looks for a cause. He will pin the curse on some current event in the person's life, if he can find one. But more often he will find a cause in a previous generation, and he'll use that to bring the curse to life, particularly if he can link the long-ago cause to a present-day action.

What are some of the current causes that will allow a spirit of Jezebel to take root in the here and now?

COMMON ROOTS OF JEZEBEL

Sexual Abuse

It is common to find the demon Jezebel in women who have been raped, incested, or molested. Such moral evils are virtually an automatic right for demons to actuate an ancient curse, or to enter into a woman, especially when the abuse has been committed by someone in the bloodline. My experience as an exorcist informs me that the majority of sexually abused women have a Jezebel spirt. This conclusion is not to place fault on them. Quite the contrary. I realize that it doesn't seem fair that the victim gets the demon, but Satan doesn't operate by some ill-defined rules of cosmic justice. The devil takes what he can when he can.

The demonization by a spirit of Jezebel in instances of sexual abuse is mainly due to the lack of help such victims get by counseling, therapy, or inner healing. Without proper intervention, what follows is often unresolved feelings of anger, revenge, hatred, and retribution directed toward the specific abuser and men in general. (If the victim is male, the reverse is true.)

One of the most dramatic examples of this I have personally encountered was also somewhat unusual. A middle-aged man brought his

89-year-old mother to a private Encounter session. He wheeled into the room this grandmotherly woman, seated in a wheel chair and tethered to an oxygen tank. Somewhat physically feeble, but mentally alert, she addressed me forthrightly.

"I am about to tell you something I've never told anyone," the spry woman said. "When I was four years old I was sexually molested."

The words came slowly and with deep emotional anguish. The silence of those 85 years was etched on her face and embedded in her trembling voice. All those decades she had carried this dark secret inside, burying it in some concealed corner of her soul. Could it be that a demon, more specifically Jezebel, had been hiding all this time, waiting for an opportunity to strike down this saintly woman at the end of her days?

Even though I had hunted down Jezebel hundreds of times before, I had a moment of self-doubt. Would I be able to nail this evil monarch of murder in a woman who'd spent eight decades building walls of emotional insulation to hide her intense distress? Sure, I believe and have taught that most victims of sexual abuse get a demon of Jezebel, but Patricia's case was going to be an ultimate test for my supposition.

The moment I said, "Jezebel, if you're there, I command that you come forward," Patricia's back stiffened. For a moment I thought she was going to get up from the wheelchair. Her gentle eyes hardened, and she leaned forward menacingly. In most cases, I would have assumed a physically defensive posture and alerted those with me to get ready for restraint. This was not necessary with this elderly woman, but I was surprised at how aggressively the demon responded.

"What do you want?"

"Are you Jezebel?'

"Yes!"

"When did you enter her bloodline?"

"Through sexual abuse and witchcraft three generations ago." Jezebel glared at me. "I've given her COPD, you know. She can't breathe. I told her she'll die soon."

With my cross and Bible in hand, I leaned forward to invade Jezebel's space. The demon was relaxed and confident. "I'm good," she bragged.

I glared at the demon more intently.

"I don't like you," Jezebel said. Then with a sly grin the demon added, "Why don't you go away?"

Jezebel knew that wasn't going to happen, but by some demonic logic, why not try?

"I'm not going anywhere," I retorted, "but you are."

"You can't make me," Jezebel insisted.

Of course, I did make Jezebel leave. But not without a fight, as much as could be mustered from an elderly woman in a wheelchair.

The obstinacy of this demon, even in an aged body, was remarkable. The fact that Jezebel was still feisty and unwilling to release her victim is worth noting. In a practical sense, there wasn't much that the demon could do to further any evil intentions in this case. But it was enough to torment this poor, old soul just for the satisfaction of it. Jezebel was simply being Jezebel. The demon had maintained its hold because of unconfessed sexual victimization and wasn't going anywhere unless made to leave.

Rejection by a Father

God has given special purpose to the role of fatherhood, especially when it affects female children. I should know. I have three daughters. And at one point, they were all teenagers at the same time. (I can almost hear the groans of sympathy from my readers.) In truth, they are wonderful, young women. But I've seen personally illustrated in my own family dynamic the important role a father plays in affirming biblical manhood to children, especially during the developmental ages. It's my wife who teaches them how to be godly women, but it's my responsibility, as well as I can, to teach them how a man treats a women. The female child without an adequate understanding of fatherly love is possible prey for Jezebel. When a father-daughter relationship is dysfunctional, perhaps even physically, emotionally, or sexually damaging, Jezebel exploits several weaknesses.

Hatred of Men

A man-hating woman will act in a Jezebel-like manner. That in itself sets the stage for demonization. A bad dad may reflect all that a child knows about maleness. Unless there are uncles or grandparents or other godly men around who mitigate the message of negative behavior, this may be the only role model the female child may ever see of male-female interaction. If a five-year-old, for example, can't trust her emotions or body with her own father, what man could she ever trust?

Hating men quickly turns into hurting men. And a women who instinctively wants to hurt men will drive them to inappropriate behavior which further enforces the characterization that men are evil. As a case in point, a father who has negatively sexualized his daughter through incest or improper moral behavior will set her up to find a bad man like daddy. (It is uncanny, but that is often how the pathology of negative behavior works.) When she has a relationship with, or marriage to, that bad man, if he doesn't already have a problem with pornography (as an example) he may develop one. The woman will think, "I told you so," and a vicious cycle is set in motion; the male partner acts badly, the Jezebel spirit hates him for doing it, and it drives him further away with the likelihood that his sin problem will become worse. Jezebel convinces her female victim that all her negative assumptions about men were right. So, the only way to get, keep, or survive with a male partner is to deceive and dominate them. And it's done the same way daddy did it, with sex or devious emotional regulation.

The Men-Are-Only-Interested-In-One-Thing Syndrome

The absence of paternal tenderness and connection may leave a daughter thinking that what's really important to men is her physical assets. Consequently, the first few males to come along will be seen as prey to entice and conquer with lust. The role of exploiting then easily leads to being exploited, which reinforces the negative image of men. Sex becomes a means of getting the upper hand in the relationship. Mutual pleasure and emotional bonding mean nothing. Jezebel may also push the relationship beyond the boundaries of mutual satisfaction to deviant kinds of sexuality, such as sadomasochism and other violent or kinky experimentation.

I recall well one particular case of a well-known, successful minister who saw me at the urging of his wife. Only a few minutes into the session, the wife broke down and sobbed, "My husband makes me watch X-rated videos with him. Then he expects me to sexually perform what we've been watching. At first I went along with it for the sake of our marriage, which was shaky. I thought that if I could become more sexually satisfying to my husband that it would save our marriage and ministry. Now I just feel degraded and humiliated." Her eyes flashed with anger. She looked right at her husband, a man of God who preached to thousands from his pulpit and added, "I hate him. I don't even care about the marriage any more. I just want out of this moral sickness!"

Jezebel had done a good job of ruining this marriage and ministry. Jezebel in the woman (she had been sexually molested as a child) partnered with Jezebel in this Christian leader (yes, powerful and anointed men of God can have demons) for an unholy alliance from hell. The wife's abuse as a child made her somewhat tentative in the bedroom. Unfortunately, this pastor aggressively taught that Christians can't be affected by demons so there was no way to get deliverance for his wife. Instead of helping her to receive healing and deliverance, he turned to depraved, sexual stimulation for a solution. The wife's childhood horror came back to haunt her. All over again she was being abused by a man, reinforcing the twisted convention in her mind that men were all about sex and only sex. Both husband and wife had Jezebel spirits, a clever plot that made helping them most difficult. Sadly, the husband refused to accept the idea that both he and his wife had opened demonic doors to spiritual oppression, and he never followed up after our encounter.

There Aren't Any Good Men

This narrative is a self-fulfilling prophecy. If daddies are bad, then all men must be bad. Finding a good man is a hopeless pursuit. Dumb down your expectations. And if the man you partner with or married treats you badly, that's to be expected. Learn to live with it or find a way to get control, by outright domination or artful relationship management.

It's the God-given goal of a biblical father to be the kind of man that he wants his daughter(s) to marry. The greatest compliment any daughter could pay a father is to say, "I married a man just like you, Dad." That's not to attribute to fathers some unrealistic perfection; but in the Christian community we need to encourage fatherly role models that by words and actions mirror the kind of man a godly woman will want. That goal leaves less room for Jezebel to maneuver.

That ideal is very tall order for any Christian father, but with God's grace it is possible. On the contrary, the sure way to make a daughter a target for a Jezebel spirit is to mistreat that child in any number of ways and incline her to think that, in the falsely despairing words of the old song: "A good man is hard to find; you always get the other kind. Just when you think that he's your pal, you look for him and find him fooling around with some other gal."

A FINAL THOUGHT ABOUT JEZEBEL'S OPEN DOORS

Always keep in mind that no evil spirit, not even Jezebel, can arbitrarily torment an individual. There must be an open door, whether generational or current. In this chapter I've mentioned just a few contemporary circumstances that facilitate the oppression of Jezebel. There are, of course, many more. To get Jezebel out and keep her out, it's important to identify what she feeds on in the here and now. This requires more than a bombastic power encounter with this demon. The competent minister who seeks to banish Jezebel will take time to see what hidden hurts and dysfunction in the host's past gave a way for this evil spirit to wheedle her way in. Then, that deeply buried hurt or wrongful way of thinking must be healed and mended. This careful ministry of prayer and spiritual therapy will destroy the foundation of Jezebel's entrenchment. The freed individual can then truly get free and live free.

Chapter 11

JEZEBEL'S ARROGANT ANTICS

As a longtime minister of deliverance I feel that I am adequately knowledgeable on how to recognize and respond to Jezebel in a way that weakens and defeats this demon. I don't claim to know all there is to understand about this diabolical force, but I have deciphered some strategies which have proven to be effective against Jezebel. Here are some characteristics of this evil spirit that provide guidelines to confronting and conquering, by God's grace and power, this most pernicious of demons.

ARROGANCE AND PRIDE

During times of deliverance it is relatively easy to spot the evil spirit Jezebel. Arched eyebrows, head slightly askance, overbearing arrogance, and insolent self-confidence—that is Jezebel. Jezebel is also a spirit of witchcraft, and according to First Samuel 15:23, witchcraft is rebellion. ("For rebellion is as the sin of witchcraft.") Besides Lucifer, in my experience as an exorcist, no demon displays more pride than does Jezebel.

Pride makes Jezebel strong, but pride also makes Jezebel weak. Jezebel has massive doses of overconfidence, and that often leads to her downfall. She frequently overplays her hand. Like an athlete who loses his edge as a result of winning so many times, Jezebel has conquered innumerable foes, and she thinks she is invincible. Jezebel's haughtiness is her downfall.

I am of the school of thought that believes demons can and should be interrogated verbally. How else can the most insidious of Satan's schemes be uncovered? While the minister of deliverance must never engage in trivial conversation or be misled by extraneous information, a focused questioning of demons, in this case Jezebel, can be helpful. It fills in missing pieces of the spiritual puzzle that leads to removing all the legal rights of an invading evil spirit. Using this paradigm of deliverance is especially effective with the Jezebel spirit. Take, for example, the following actual exchange between me and a certain Jezebel demon. I began my taunt to provoke the evil spirit which initially refused to converse.

"This woman you've possessed has had a tough time. You've made her life hell—molested as a child, raped as a teenager, constantly put down by her mother. Bet you're proud of that, aren't you, Jezebel?"

Smirk. A toss of the head backward with jaw jutting out in defiance.

"Oh, c'mon, Jezebel, you know you've made her life miserable."

Pursed lips. Narrowed eyes. Intense stare.

"As a demon, you've done a good job. But do you have a legal right to continue tormenting her?"

Arms crossed in defiance. Sense of satisfaction.

"Well, do you have a legal right?"

Broad grin. "No, but it doesn't make any difference. She's mine, and I'm going to keep her."

Now drawn out from hiding into a verbal exchange, Jezebel is still smug. I get a bit more intense.

100

"Yes or no. Do you have a legal right?"

A bit too cocky as a result of hearing how much she has tormented her host, Jezebel now presses the issue. "No, but I'm not leaving."

A threshold has been crossed. Jezebel is now engaged in a back-and-forth exchange that will eventually trip her up.

Now, taking an offensive stance: "If you had a legal right you'd say so. You're only there because no one has exposed your strongholds in this woman's life. How did you get there?"

Snarl. Curled lip and hands tensed in a claw-like fashion.

"Her father gave her to me as a child when he raped her! This woman doesn't even remember it."

Silence for a moment. Jezebel knows she has said too much. She has just given away the root of the sexual curse that led to so much misery. Jezebel is smart. Coy. But, as I said, full of pride. Her bragging has just been her undoing, in this particular case.

What followed next was the typical exchange that I have described in my training videos and in our International School of Exorcism training procedures. But in most cases when dealing with Jezebel, the revelatory information necessary to remove demonic legal rights will likely not come forth until Jezebel is drawn into the open. Appealing to Jezebel's arrogance can often be the key.

SEDUCTION

This particular characteristic is the one most often associated with Jezebel. Whore. Slut. Seductress. Man-eater on the prowl. But Jezebel's enticement isn't always sexual. That is the most common way that Jezebel wends her way into a marriage or a church, but not always. The persuasion she uses takes many forms and has many tentacles. Consider this scenario from my archives of exorcisms.

A man named Ron was afflicted by demons of Infirmity and Destruction. Everything he set his hands to failed, and one disease after another weakened him physically. Ron knew that there was much unsavory behavior in his family's background. But until we provoked his demons to tell us factually what happened, he had no idea regarding the immensity of evil in his ancestral bloodline. After we pressured the demons to reveal why Ron had suffered so many setbacks and diseases in his life, the demon revealed there was a curse of infidelity going back four generations.

"His great-great-great-grandmother had an affair," the demon of Destruction boasted. "She used every trick she had to seduce another woman's husband. That was all we needed."

Granted, adultery is a serious moral failure, but that didn't seem to be enough evil to warrant what Ron had suffered. There had to be more. I challenged Destruction.

"So, that's bad, but not that bad, compared to what this man has been through."

Destruction took the bait. He was proud of what he'd done. "Of course not," the spirit said almost casually. "It was the murder that sealed it for us."

"Murder?"

"When the wife found out what happened, she arranged for someone to poison that adulteress's food. But not before..."

There was a quick shift in demeanor. I knew another demon had surfaced, and experience taught me who it was.

"Murder! Come to attention!"

The evil spirt snapped erect as if a ramrod had been forced into its back. "So, now you know our little secret," Murder cackled.

I wasn't sure that was the only secret. "And before the woman was murdered?"

The demon knew I wasn't taking such a simple crime as the final answer to Ron's torment. I pressed my Cross of Deliverance against the demon's forehead.

"Rite," Murder screamed.

"Right? Do you mean legal right?"

"No, you foolish human. Scottish rite. Freemasonry. This man's ancestor was contacted by Freemasons who offered to abort the baby resulting from the affair. She got pregnant, you know. It was murder in the Lodge that gave us the power we needed."

A less experienced deliverance minister might have stopped there and gone on to attempt expelling the spirit. Spiritual discernment told me that there was still more.

"Murder, are you the Strong Man, the Chief?'

"No!"

"Then whoever is the chief spirit attacking this man?"

The mannerisms of Murder and Destruction gave way to an even more evil presence

"Lucifer?"

"He's above me. I'm Jupiter. I go back to the adulterous woman's English ancestors who adopted the gods of the Romans. They worshiped me as if they worshiped the sun. You should have seen how Zeus and I used to get along."

"Who cares," I interjected, stopping the unnecessary flow of demonic babble. "I demand that Lucifer come to attention."

Instantly the chief of demons looked at me.

"Are you alone? You usually have someone like Moloch with you. After all, a baby was sacrificed."

Lucifer let out a hearty, demonic laugh. "He's here, along with Baal."

"No doubt. Those two are usually together."

I paused and stared down Lucifer. I knew who he was hiding. Her fingerprints were all over this particular possession. Lust, fornication, adultery, and seduction.

"You wouldn't be hiding Jezebel, would you?"

"She was the one who planned the whole affair. That foolish man. He just thought he was getting a little sex on the side. He had no idea that he was a pawn in our little game. That man would never have committed adultery on his own without Jezebel's help. And I wouldn't be here without her."

Jezebel isn't always the most powerful demon, when compared to a Luciferian spirit or princely demons in the hierarchy of Satan's Kingdom, but she is often the most crucial factor in the evil link of a curse. In this particular case she opened the doors to demons of Murder, Infanticide, Freemasonry, Infirmity and Destruction. Without Jezebel's ability to seduce, much suffering and death might have been averted.

Ron's exorcism was successful, but not without a strenuous fight. Jezebel turned out to be the most formidable foe in the pantheon of demons, even more difficult to dislodge than Lucifer. Today, Ron is much improved and getting back his health and his life. But he was nearly destroyed. And it was all because of a sexual escapade more than 100 years ago, both participants compelled by Jezebel and her seductive ways.

SEDUCTION, JEZEBEL-STYLE

How does Jezebel seduce? Forget those images evoked by strip joints and "gentlemen's clubs." Sure, Jezebel feels welcome there; but her seduction is usually more subtle. Sly is an understatement. She's usually not obvious. Sometimes she is downright spiritual. If transparent sexual lust were Jezebel's primary motif, that would be obvious. But beware the Jezebel person who longs for attention and has deep emotional needs that her partner isn't meeting. She forms a bond of mutuality. As she seeks her needs to be met she also seems to meet the wants of the one being seduced. She may be kind, empathetic, and understanding of others' hurts, to a point of smothering them with advice and attention.

If it seems too good to be true, it probably is, and it's also probably Jezebel. If she understands when no one else does; if she touches a place in your heart no one has, she is looking for an opening. That's not to say that all caring and kind people are Jezebels. Far from it. My point is that Jezebel takes what is good in empathetic individuals and perverts it in her hirelings for a diabolical purpose.

One of the most interesting aspects of Jezebel's sensuality is that sex is just for the thrill of it; however it can also be a means to an end. Most women who are Jezebels before marriage or during initial courtship turn out to be frigid and emotionally aloof later. Since one of Jezebel's main entry points is sexual violation, once the prey has been captured, interest in sexual conduct wanes. Such a Jezebel person probably hates sex anyway, because it was a tool of repression or victimization. This kind of individual usually grows to hate sex because it is emotionally linked to past abuse. Consequently, Jezebel, operating in a sexual abuse victim, generally gets such a person to the place that they are little aroused by sexual foreplay once their partner/prey has been captured.

Please understand that I am not demeaning the psychological dynamics that play out in the mind of someone sexually violated. Nor am I making light of their struggles with intimacy. Quite the contrary. I am trying to emphasize that one who has been sexually violated may think of themselves, female or male, as demeaned and worthless. Sex to them has been objectified without any context of true commitment, pleasure, and intimacy. It's merely a physical act associated with emotional and physical pain; hence they may be driven by Jezebel to get even with the opposite sex, whoever the latest victim may be, by using seduction. They tease and then they torture (mentally and spiritually). Their bodies are disconnected from real sex and womanhood/manhood. Too hot to handle before marriage or engagement, they suddenly turn cold. And if Jezebel is in the mix, it's all calculated to keep the partner/spouse off balance and in a controlled, dependent position.

That is why most prostitutes are usually Jezebels, often through no part of their own. According to the most recently available statistics, 80 percent of imprisoned rapists were molested as children and 80 percent of prostitutes were sexually abused as children. My own studied observation is that more than 90 percent of sexual abuse victims are demonized, and the main spirit is almost always Jezebel.

SPIRITUALITY

It's obvious that from a historical, biblical perspective Jezebel is a religious spirit. The Jezebel of the Old Testament was all about religion, especially false religion. Jezebel isn't an atheist. She oozes spirituality, the negative and fake kind. That's why Jezebel is found so often in the Church doing what she can to destroy the work of God. Her tactics are aimed at specific targets:

Pastors

This demon wants to bring down men and women of God. And to read the religious headlines of late, she has done pretty well. At the writing of this book, in just the past six months Jezebel has derailed or destroyed five of the most significant megachurch pastors in America. I'll defer mentioning them by name, but it is worth noting that their respective congregations numbered 20,000, 14,000, 10,000, 8,000 and 6,000. And these are only the best-known cases, because they represent some of the largest churches in America.

There have been countless other tragedies of pastors of smaller churches. What's interesting to me is that each of these men abdicated as a result of sexual moral failure, and each of them vehemently opposed teachings such as the ones found in this book. None believed in deliverance and all taught that Christians can't be demonized. What a set-up for Jezebel. If the man in the pulpit denies that there is a Jezebel spirit, to which even men of God might be susceptible, that's the perfect cover under which this demon can operate.

Pastor's Wives

I am not ignoring the fact that there are women in spiritual leadership who fall victim to Jezebel just as men do. I've dealt with them too. But for practical purposes we'll devote our attention to the main targets of the Jezebel spirit: male pastors and their wives. Jezebel particularly hates the godly pastor's wife. She doesn't so much try to lead her into sexual sin, though it does happen, as much as she tries to undercut the wife's position in the church. Remember, Jezebel is religious and wants to be right next to the pastor in everything he does.

There is no length to which a Jezebel woman will not sacrifice and labor to ingratiate herself in a responsible and needed role in the church. Now, don't jump to conclusions that this profile automatically fits some woman that you know in your church now. There are many dedicated and selfless women who rise to leadership positions because of their spiritual gifts. But when you see such a woman fail to defer to the pastor's wife or, worse yet, subtly say demeaning things about her, look out. Jezebel wants to supplant the pastor's wife and play the role of a quasi-spiritual advisor and confident. Her ultimate aim is to replace the spiritual mission of the pastor's wife and be the pastor's main source of advice and consent.

Spiritual Role Model

Jezebel isn't interested in bringing the world into the church. She wants to foment prophecies, healings, miracles, revelations, even deliverance—so long as these spiritual phenomena are under her control and she can corrupt them. In fact, Jezebel sometimes appears to be the most spiritual woman in the church. She is full of spiritual insights, prophetic words, and even discerning advice. The tricky part is that the Jezebel spirits tries to latch on to a truly anointed, spiritual woman (men too, but for sake of description and not due to gender prejudice we'll focus on the female conduit of Jezebel). Jezebel then attempts to corrupt such a person. If Jezebel can't have a vessel totally corrupted from the beginning she will look for someone who is well-meaning and gifted with a spiritual destiny and try to pervert that person's calling.

MORE ON JEZEBEL IN THE CHURCH

Once Jezebel is successful with her recruitment of her human vehicle of subversion, she will make certain that this individual operates in secret. She'll be accountable to no one, not even the pastor, whom she often undercuts with tenuous tactics. Like a spiritual butterfly she flits from ear to ear in the congregation speaking words that question the pastor's authority and leadership. It may be his sermons, his clothes, his car, his home, his salary, his leisure time, his theology, his whatever that she picks on. And she often seeks no official positon in the church. That way there is no accountability. She is a spiritual vagabond, creating havoc wherever she turns.

Sometimes these women are used by Jezebel unknowingly. They may even be deluded into thinking that they are doing the right thing. Some live with unresolved pain in their past from which they haven't been healed. Without receiving prayer for inner healing and deliverance, their spiritual gifts become corrupted.

SOME CONCLUDING THOUGHTS

These characteristics of arrogance, seduction and spirituality are by no means the only characteristics defining the Jezebel spirit. Later in the book we'll consider more; but these primary distinguishing features serve as an alert to possible activity of this evil spirit. Later, we will also give advice on how to counter Jezebel's attributes. But if the reader were only to be armed against these aspects mentioned above, the battle against this age-old evil would be on the way to being won.

Chapter 12

JEZEBEL: LOVER OF
YOUR SOUL

*Reader's Note: The following contains sensitive sexual information
and should not be read by minors without parental consent.*

THE WOMAN WHO SCHEDULED A PERSONAL SPIRITUAL ENCOUNTER
session with me, a one-on-one in-depth spiritual analysis, was nervous
and obviously somewhat reluctant. Even though she had spent considerable time and money to travel from afar to meet with me, there was
hesitation in her body language and voice. I conduct hundreds of such
session each year and it's often apparent when I first speak with the
individual whether or not they are comfortable with such a meeting.
Often individuals schedule time with me out of exasperation. Things
are so bad in their lives, the spiritual oppression is so acute, that they
realize drastic action is needed. Exorcism and deliverance may be the
intervention of necessity.

I often begin Encounter sessions by quoting to people the words of
Jesus in John 8:32—"The truth shall make you free." Only by giving

full disclosure of every relevant spiritual issue in their lives can I help. What they tell me may be uncomfortable. I emphasize that I often hear people say, "I've never told this to anyone before."

I look at then intently and say, "If you hold back I can't help you. If there is a dark secret of your past, I have to know about it. Any place possible that Satan could hide in your soul must be exposed.

As my wife points out many times, *To heal, you must reveal.*

Once I feel that the one seeking help is at ease, I begin with probing questions to find out where the devil has embedded himself in undisclosed shame. Gradually, the pain begins to pour out of their soul. Some weep. Others express frustration or anger as they release pent-up feelings. I've learned to tell when they are holding back and as gently as possible encourage them to speak with full disclosure. At some point the hurts are released and the horrible stories of unimaginable evil seep out of the cracks in the individual's otherwise calm and collected façade.

They tell me about incest the family has hidden; about sexual molestation swept under the carpet to save face; about spiritual neglect and the most devastating things that have been said to them—sometimes by their own parents when growing up. But a significant portion of people, usually women, start to talk about demonic sexual contact. They begin with oblique language and skirt the real issue out of embarrassment. They use code words and euphemisms because the sexual context is too sensitive to express. Some have grown up in prudish homes where even the word "sex" was forbidden. So, for these women (men too but since most victims are women we'll focus on them) the frank discussion of any kind of sexual behavior is like a visit to a dental surgeon who has not offered any analgesics.

Eventually they blurt it out with phrases like: "Something touched me." "I felt a hand on my leg." "It seemed like someone was lying next to me." "I could hear breathing and sensed the presence of someone in my bedroom."

Some even get right to the issue by saying: "I don't know if I was asleep or awake, but it felt like someone or something was having sex with me." A few are even blunter: "It felt as if something was physically penetrating me, and my body experienced a sexual response."

First, some background on the phenomenon known variously as incubus, succubus, or alternately as a "spiritual husband" or "spiritual wife."

THE IDEA OF SEX WITH DEMONS

In 1968, Paramount Pictures released what was to become a classic horror film: *Rosemary's Baby*. Mia Farrow played a pregnant woman who feared that her actor husband had made a deal with the devil. In exchange for movie stardom, her child would be a devil baby destined for sacrifice. She undergoes a visionary experience in which, the night she conceives her child, she is raped by a demon in front of her husband. Rosemary is later told that, during labor, her baby died. She eventually learns the baby is alive and is the spawn of Satan. The movie was written and directed by Roman Polanski, whose own wife, Sharon Tate, was murdered by the Charles Manson family when she was eight-and-a-half months pregnant—the year after *Rosemary's Baby* was released.

The phenomenon of demonic conjugation, usually known as incubus/succubus or "spiritual wife/husband," is either dramatically increasing or participants are more willing to speak of it. In my seminars and Personal Encounter sessions, the topic comes up more and more; therefore, it's important to know what it is and how to address the matter in a counseling and inner healing ministry context. Understandably, it's a touchy topic that some might think is more suited for private discussion, not a public forum. My reason for bringing this subject into the open is to let those who suffer know that they are not alone, and that there is hope and help. I'm also intent on confronting the Jezebel spirit behind this evil. The demon Incubus/Succubus usually works in concert with the demon Jezebel.

Indeed, the idea of sex with demons is as old as antiquity. Incubus, from the Latin "incubo," to "lie upon," occurs when a demon takes on male substance to cohabit with a woman. The female opposite is called succubus. Though the subject is taboo in Christian circles, that has not always been so. St. Augustine dealt with the subject in his book, *The City of God,* in which the Church Father stated, "There is also a very general rumor. Many have verified it by their own experience and trustworthy persons have corroborated the experience others told, that sylvans and fauns, commonly called incubi, have often made wicked assaults upon women."

Although Western cultures are skittish about such topics, I find that those of African and Caribbean descent are much more open. They also seem to be more victimized. The marriage of women and men to "spiritual" spouses as an introduction to sexuality is more widespread in these cultures.

Take the example of a woman named Mary, who came from Ghana. She had no qualms about telling our prayer team about her experiences with a "spiritual husband." It started when she was a child, pre-puberty. At the time she had no idea what was happening or even that she was being molested. As she grew older, the activity was more intense with her demon lover demanding to be satisfied several times a week. It became a way of life until Mary became a Christian in her late teens. Then the attacks became more vicious. Satan, now threatened that he would lose his cohabitant, intensified the demonic attacks. She would awaken at night being pinned to the bed unable to move. Not one but several demons had their way with her. She was told that they "owned" her body because of a ritual when she was a baby.

Her mother had taken her to a fetish priest for a sea-water bath to "protect" against evil spirits. The priest/witch doctor cut a piece of Mary's hair and tied it to a locket. Her mother was told that as long as Mary had this amulet around her neck she'd be safe. In reality, this locket was a talisman ceding spiritual legal rights to the demons of the witch doctor. Now, as a young adult, she still suffered these hideous attacks, though with less frequency since she learned how to pray them away.

During my exorcism of Mary I cut to the chase and went straight for Jezebel, who manifested easily. The spiritual legal rights of the infant dedication to the devil were renounced and Jezebel was bound to Incubus and both expelled in the Name of Jesus. The demonic attacks stopped instantly, and Mary now rests peacefully each night. Sadly, it had taken some years for her to find me, someone who would understand and not disgrace her further with uneasy rejection of her graphic stories of sexual assault.

Whether in the context of a spirit/female cohabiting with a human male or a spirit/male cohabiting with a human female, the ultimate danger of supernatural sex is getting a demon. I've done hundreds of exorcisms on such individuals and can testify that this form of possession is hideous and difficult to overcome. Yielding one's body to a ghostly lover is an open door to demonization of the soul.

I also raise this subject because of its recent notoriety in Hollywood. Kasha, a singer/song writer/rapper, claims to have had sex with a "ghost," described in her song "Supernatural." She explained the song by saying, "It's about experiences with the supernatural, but in a sexy way. I had a couple of [sexual] experiences with the supernatural. He was a ghost. I'm very open to it." According to one respected report, Lucy Liu, of "Ally McBeal" fame and starring in the CBS-TV show "Elementary" has indulged in this practice, as has Paz de la Huerta of "Boardwalk Empire" fame. And these outspoken actresses may only be the tip of a new trend among female, and presumably also male, stars.

My warning to anyone contemplating sexual experimentation with such evil, spurred on by these stars, is that your nocturnal ghostly lover wants more than your body. He wants your soul, not for a journey of sexual ecstasy, but for a one-way trip to hell.

HELPING THOSE WHO HAVE SUFFERED DEMONIC SEXUAL ASSAULT

Those in deliverance or healing ministry who confront this evil will find few if any resources on how to handle this taboo topic. Here are some brief thoughts on dealing with this issue from the perspective of ministering to victims of demonic sexual molestation:

- Be careful about further shaming. The individual will likely have heavy doses of false guilt which any further condemnation won't help dissipate.

- Find out if the issue is generational, if any other family members have been victimized.

- All sexual sin must be renounced and all ungodly relationships ended. The demon may have been sexually transferred and that link must be severed.

- If a ritual or emotional marriage to this entity occurred, there must be a spiritual divorce, particularly if the cohabitant has been viewed as a "spiritual husband or wife."

- Any pornography or sexual devices most be destroyed immediately. Whatever aroused the fantasies must be avoided.

- Since many such episodes occur in dreaming or nocturnal states, defensive praying when going to bed is essential; have the victim take a holy object to bed, such as a Bible or cross.

- There may be past involvement in the occult that opened the door, such as beliefs in spiritual lovers or alien cohabitation; have the victim renounce all such beliefs.

- If the person is unmarried, they should remain chaste while going through deliverance; if married, their spouse must claim "one-flesh" authority over any such spiritual adultery.

- Be careful to distinguish between psychosis and genuine episodes of demonic sexuality; this is difficult since such experiences are so surreal, they dwell in parts of the imagination where fact and fantasy are sometimes blurred. Beware the individual who claims such experiences as the result of repressed sexual thoughts which haven't been properly processed.

- All self-induced sexual arousal must stop as this will invite further oppression.

- Exorcism is necessary in most genuine cases; the most common demons encountered are Jezebel, Incubus, Succubus, Spiritual Rape, Spiritual Husband/Wife, Lilith.

We shall not at this point deal with questions of whether this is analogous to the human/demon cohabitation some think is referred to in Genesis, chapter 6. That is a matter for later consideration in this book. This is also not the time or place to discuss the controversy of whether demons are capable of inseminating humans and thus producing hybrid, half-human/half-demon offspring, so-called spawns of the devil. The purpose of this chapter is to get the subject of demonic cohabitation out of the closet and into the counseling or ministry setting as a topic of frank discussion when needed.

A WORD FOR COUNSELORS AND DELIVERANCE MINISTERS

A word is in order for those who are professional counselors or deliverance ministers. If a woman comes to you with accounts of waking or going to sleep and feeling paralyzed and pinned to the bed, don't dismiss it as mere "sleep paralysis." Psychologists who have encountered this phenomenon describe it as a transitional state between waking and sleep. It is supposedly accompanied by muscle atonia, weakness. Psychiatrists may try to link it to sleep apnea, narcolepsy, or various anxiety and PTSD disorders.

I concur that some episodes of sleep paralysis may have a psychological explanation. Other cases are too clearly demonic to ignore the spiritual assumptions. The truth is that there is an extensive medical history of individuals who believe that an intruder has attempted suffocation or even strangulation in the midst of the sexual invasion. Neurological literature has highly sophisticated explanations for the phenomenon involving theories of dysfunctional REM sleep and other pathophysiological interpretations.

Indeed, some of these conclusions may be valid in certain cases, especially the idea that the sufferer is in a dissociative state. (Please consult our other books and DVDs for teaching on Dissociative Identity Disorder.) This concept has spiritual ramifications. Suppose that an individual, because of sexual abuse, has an alter-ego personality that believes the lie that they are destined for abuse. That "alter" may have formed a demonic soul bound with an evil spirit, a Jezebel/Incubus demon, believing that the demon has a right to sexual bonding. In the states between wakefulness and sleep this alter may permit Incubus conjugation, only to have the person's core state of consciousness become more fully awake and thus be terrorized by the Satanic attack which had been allowed by the alter.

Various cultures have legends of hags, the *pisadeira* (Brazil), shadow people, or the "witch is riding you" (voodoo societies). European and Scandinavian countries have many legends of succubi and goblins. The "Ogun Oru" is a common African belief in demonic nighttime infestation of the body. Are we to presume that this ubiquitous belief in demons sexually assaulting people can be explained away as tribal myths or neurological malfunctions? Keep in mind that the word "nightmare" comes from the word *mare*, the name of demonic beings in early Germanic cultures. In fact sleep paralysis was first referred to by the word "nightmare."

It does no good for Christian pastors and counselors to immediately assume that someone with a tale of nocturnal sexual encounters has a mental or physiological problem better treated by the medical community. The increasing incidence of this dilemma is a clear indication that Jezebel is working overtime to take advantage of a sexualized society where abuse is rampant. As Christians, we of all people should be in the forefront of ministering to those who have been victimized by Jezebel's cohorts, Incubus and Succubus.

Chapter 13

SHE'S EVERYWHERE,
EVERYWHERE

ANYONE INVOLVED IN DELIVERANCE MINISTRY IS AWARE OF JEZEBEL'S ubiquity. It is de rigueur for this demon to show up almost on cue. Nearly 50 percent of my exorcism caseload involves confronting Jezebel as the chief spirit or one of the main players in the dismantling of a possession process. "It's you, again," is Jezebel's standard line of introduction when I pray for people and Jezebel presents herself.

"Yes, and I'm here to do to you what the Lord and I have always done to you before, send you back to the Abyss where you belong!"

The disdain is mutual. "I know you," my old spiritual nemesis often adds. I suspect that other deliverance ministers who operate with any frequency in this realm have the same experience. Many have told me so.

Why? I've asked that question over and over. I'm still not entirely certain of the answer, but I do have some theories; but before laying out my thoughts, consider these observations. Here are a dozen characteristics of Jezebel that represent her constant presence, or at least give that illusion.

JEZEBEL IS CROSS-CULTURAL

I've ministered in over 100 countries of the world, and I have found that Jezebel is everywhere, though her permutations may differ slightly, depending on the cultural context. She may be found under a different name, but she always typifies the same concept and function. Ethnicity or national origin of the host do not seem to be limiting factors for Jezebel's spiritual occupation of a victim. This is truly a cross-cultural evil force.

For example, when I discover a woman has been sexually abused, whether it's in South Africa or Australia, Russia or Canada, Jezebel is usually present somewhere in that individual's demonic system. There are certain behavioral aspects that represent the style of this demon: perversion, pornography, sexual abuse and dysfunction, spiritual infiltration, relational domination, to name a few. When these are present, Jezebel is close by no matter what the geographical location.

Generally speaking, evil spirits only have locational specificity when it facilitates their assignment. For example, if their responsibility is to bring about war or bloodshed in a particular area of the globe, they will adapt to the cultural and historical characteristic of that particular nation. If the country is an aggressor, Jezebel will predominate. If the country is under attack, an Ahab spirit may encourage unreasonable conciliation. The whole idea is keep the conflict going and for evil and bloodshed to prevail.

JEZEBEL IS AN END-TIMES DEMON

It is clear from John's Revelation that the Thyatira church is a prophetic peek at times as they appear to be now (see Rev. 2), as is the Laodicea church (see Rev. 3). An increase in Jezebel's activity is anticipated at the end of the ages because "as it was in the days of Noah so it will be" (Luke 17:26). At the time of the Great Flood I suspect that Jezebel's predecessors (as described earlier in this book) were as active as this demon is pervasive today.

Has Jezebel been as frequently encountered before in deliverance ministry? That's hard to evaluate. The spiritual phenomenon of exorcism has, unfortunately, been little historically documented in a systematic and credible fashion. Compared to other theological topics, the literature is paltry. With scant historical data to go by, we are left to base opinions on largely contemporary, empirical evidence. And that evidence tells me that Jezebel's activities are increasing as we near the return of Christ.

When will the coming of Christ occur? That, of course, is open to much speculation. What we do know in general is that there will be an explosion of knowledge (see Dan 12:4). An unprecedented (except for the judgment of Sodom—see Luke 17:29) increase in immoral behavior will overtake the entire world. A crisis of faith, instability, and apostasy will infect the Christian Church (see 2 Thess. 2:3). Persistent war and bloodshed will be endemic on a worldwide scale (see Mark 13:7). Observationally, from the perspective of my active ministry spanning nearly 40 years, these conditions just cited are, both quantitatively and qualitatively, far more significant within religion and culture than they were just a few decades ago. The decline and spiritual atrophy of formerly Christian cultures is also accelerating at an ever faster rate. If we aren't close to the end of time, we are at least significantly closer; near enough to conclude that Jezebel's intensity should be also be escalating.

JEZEBEL IS HIGHLY ADAPTABLE

In the realms of spiritual warfare, a murder demon is just that. The same with an evil spirit of, say, rejection or anger, or witchcraft. These minions of Satan function basically in the realm of their identifiable characteristics. But Jezebel can be everywhere because she is lots of things. We have detailed some of these common peculiarities in this book—control, manipulation, false spirituality—as cases in point.

This demon can be sophisticated or debased, intellectual or crude—all depending on the context of operation. Not so with most other demons. A demon of Abandonment basically operates in that arena of human misery. A demon of Death is always intent on killing the host. A demon of Deception traffics in lies. An Antichrist spirit focuses on corrupting theological truth. But Jezebel is a shape-shifter, adapting to circumstances and individuals. She can be as sweet as pie or as menacing as a savage wildcat.

Jezebel is often sensual, but can also be legalistically puritanical. Jezebel may exhibit strongly controlling characteristics, but is sometimes the author of spiritual confusion. Jezebel is usually defiant and "in your face," but I've also seen this demon manifest in a cunningly subtle manner. The manipulation of Jezebel is one of her most common activities, but she can at times appear to be very compliant, while working her ways of subversion behind a mask of false, obligatory consent. She may advocate rampant sexuality or hide under the guise of moral temperance (see 1 Tim. 4:3). Now you see her; now you don't. She perpetually plays spiritual hide-and-seek with anyone attempting to disclose her activities.

JEZEBEL INFESTS SEXUALITY

I've commented on this before, but need to expand on this as one of her many wiles. Bondage. Sadomasochism. Pornography. Voyeurism. Prostitution. Perversion. Polygamy. Polyamory. Fifty or more shades of sexual experimentation give Jezebel the go-ahead in our culture.

While it is a mistake to always think of Jezebel as synonymous with eroticism, sexual misconduct is a place she frequently inhabits. She both compels it and exploits it. Sexual immorality which leads to elective abortion allows Moloch (the ancient demon god of infant blood sacrifice) to enter. And where Moloch is, Baal and Jezebel follow. Going back to Lilith, we must remember that her role has always been as consort and conjugal deceiver.

In the Garden, Jezebel wanted sexual rights to Adam. Thwarted by God's creation of Eve, she has never given up on destroying the created and God-ordained natural order of sexuality. In whatever way possible, Jezebel mentally and theologically seduces those who are willing to concur with her sexual agenda. Nowhere is this more apparent than in the exponentially increasing crime of childhood sexual abuse. Quoting statistics is a bit misleading because the augmentation is so rapid year by year. As of the publication of this book, according to *reported* data of the National Center for Victims of Crime, approximately one-third of all youth in the United States have been sexually victimized by the age of 18. For females that is closer to 50 percent. I repeat, these statistics are based on only the *reported* cases reviewed.

About two-thirds of women abused by a family member reported that they also experienced a rape or attempted rape after the age of 14, a clear example of a generational curse in action. Most vulnerability is between the ages of seven and thirteen. Many victims were raised in a single-parent household or grew up in a home where domestic violence was rampant. According to the *Journal of Adolescent Health,* compared to those with no history of sexual abuse, young males who had been violated were five times more likely to cause teen pregnancy.

Add to all these tragic statistics two other considerations. The majority of people never tell anyone about their abuse. On an almost daily basis, some desperate soul who comes to me for healing and deliverance prayers says, "I am about to tell you something I've never told anyone before." That "something" is usually a sad, sordid tale of childhood sexual abuse. Also, add to this terrible moral toll the fact that those who have not been genitally violated may have been the victims of childhood exposure to pornography, voyeurism, and vicarious verbal improprieties. Added together, the number of those suffering is almost incalculable.

Remember, my experience indicates that almost 100 percent of these victims have been re-victimized by demonic invasion of the spirit of Jezebel. This overview settles in part the question of why those in deliverance so often run into Jezebel. If hedonism and sexual licentiousness describe the present moral climate, then it is to be expected that the spirit of Ahab's wife is more active than ever.

JEZEBEL TARGETS THE CHURCH

Since one of Jezebel's main purposes is the destruction of true worship, you'll find Jezebel haunting the precincts of religion, even fervent worship of God. Jezebel especially likes to be found behind priestly robes and thunderous pulpits. What better place to subvert God's word and purposes? This is where those who have heard of the "Jezebel Spirit" usually associate her activities. The term is mainly recognized within Pentecostal and charismatic theological communities, although not exclusively. At least in those precincts the topic has been discussed. While I'm grateful that those of a more "Spirit-filled" orientation at least broach the subject of Jezebel, they don't always get it right. They tend to focus on the areas that most interest them theologically, namely the prophetic, healing and deliverance, preaching and teaching.

The Prophetic

Revelatory utterances of various kinds are recognized as a realm where Jezebel can operate, as I've discussed previously in this book. True. Any time individuals are self-proclaimed "seers" or mouthpieces of the Lord, the subjective nature of such utterances begs for the possibility of deception and corruption. When proper guidelines of personal purity, submission to authority, and consistency of authenticity are not enforced, Jezebel can certainly run wild with all kinds of erroneous proclamations. The individual to whom the Lord is always "speaking a word," which that person tends to indiscriminately profess to others (often without much wisdom or sensitivity), may be open to the deception of Jezebel. When someone says "the Lord has a word from me to you" that "word" needs to be carefully considered before assuming automatically it is authentic and accurate. John warned in Revelation 2:20 that Jezebel (in this case a literal person who personified a kind of spiritual error in general) was a self-declared "prophetess" whose mission was to "teach" (instruct in error) and sexually "seduce" (commit "fornication") her followers.

What is to be done if it can be objectively, spiritually discerned that a Jezebel is in the midst of a congregation? First, don't go on a witch hunt to condemn those with whom others may merely have personal differences. Proper church governance procedures need to be followed to handle such a serious accusation. But don't let an infraction of this nature to continue without discipline. If it is a Jezebel spirit at work, it's a spiritual cancer that will metastasize and pollute greater and greater portions of the congregation of believers. Whatever you do, don't "leave this matter for the Lord to judge" because you may think that confronting Jezebel will upset some folks. When that's the case, then Jezebel's power grab has already gone too far.

Healing and Deliverance

Jezebel likes to operate in the supernatural, the real and fake. Since it is the aforementioned "Spirit-filled" brethren who are more likely to be open to this area of ministry, they will come under greater attack. Jezebel's agenda is simple, when it comes to the miraculous: counterfeit, corrupt, and co-opt. This is especially true in the deliverance area. Since so few churches of any kind operate in this realm, those congregations who are brave enough to incorporate the confronting of demons into the body life of the church will come under special attack. Jezebel simply can't let any church actually do what the Lord did on a regular basis—cast out demons!

Jezebel will try to *counterfeit* the process by inspiring Jezebel-dominated individuals to claim to cast out demons faster and better than others. This gives the appearance that a Jezebel-inspired deliverance minister has more power and a closer walk with the Lord than others who may labor with the process of setting people free.

Jezebel will also try to *corrupt* by false words of wisdom or knowledge; naming spirits as being present (by "revelation") without any evidence that they are; getting an inappropriate "word from the Lord" about some personal sin in the life of the person receiving ministry; claiming knowledge of nonexistent generational sins that will lead everyone down a rabbit trail of distraction.

Jezebel may *co-opt* the entire deliverance process by taking over from other qualified and spiritually discerning individuals. One way to spot this is when the Jezebel's tactics become unnecessarily harsh and demanding toward the one receiving ministry. This spirit is usually pushy and only cares about the procedure of the deliverance process instead of being considerate of what the tormented person seeking ministry may be going through.

Preaching and Teaching

Once again, remember the Apostle John warned us that Jezebel loves to "teach." Any time a prayer team or ministry cell group has one individual who takes over and forcefully tells others what to do, especially when pastoral authority hasn't been informed, look out. It may be that this domineering man or woman is just overly-enthusiastic and lacks a tempered approach to their zeal; but it may also be a red flag that Jezebel is in the midst.

Paul admonished to "recognize" those who are in charge of church ministry and to "esteem them highly in love for their work's sake" (1 Thess. 5:13). Keep in mind that to "recognize" spiritual gifts in operation, such as preaching/teaching, means not only the positive spin given to the Thessalonians but to also be aware ("recognize") when a positon of leadership has been forced on others by a Jezebel-type. In this instance, such a person should not be esteemed but admonished!

The above examples of Jezebel's penetration into a church's spiritual life are not exhaustive. Much more could be said; but these examples are spiritual traffic signs directing the reader to other areas needing caution. I repeat—Jezebel can seem to be very "spiritual" in her intentions. John's Revelation wasn't written to a group of Freemasons or a collegiate fraternity. This was no social club that Jezebel was seeking to destroy. *It was a church*, specifically a local congregation in the city of Thyatira. All those who have charge over the flock of God (see 1 Pet. 5:3-4) need to be on guard for the wolf of Jezebel who is always lurking at the door.

JEZEBEL IS IN BOTH MEN AND WOMEN

As I've mentioned before, Jezebel is a spirit without gender prefer-ence. Though historically associated with women, no gender has the corner on control and manipulation, witchcraft and spiritual rebellion. Jezebel can just as readily be in the pulpit as the kitchen. While this is true of most demons, certain evil spirits tend to be found more in men, such Rage and Murder. Men commit more violent crimes, for example. Demons of Incest and Rape will usually affect women, since they are the more common victims of such evil. Jezebel, though more generally found in women, is an equal-opportunity tormentor. In fact, one of the more clever tricks of this demon is to operate undetected in males. I have already established the ways that feminine wiles are used by Jezebel, but let's survey, for a moment, how Jezebel displays her tactics in men.

As previously identified, the nature of Jezebel is seduction, control, manipulation etc. Why should it be surmised that women are automati-cally suited to such negative characteristics? Does the Church, especially those few congregations who are concerned about any infiltration of a Jezebel spirit, have a gender bias toward assuming that women are more susceptible to demonic corruption? (You know, the old "Eve sinned first" prejudice.) Believe me, my lifetime of experience with churches and pas-tors testifies that Jezebel is alive and well in the pastorate and leadership of many churches which are male-dominated—especially those who openly discriminate against women in ministry positions.

I may just have hit a raw nerve, so hear me out. Remember the prin-ciple we've established previously. *All demons are male.* Evil spirits only assume female identities to work their evil; also, the Jezebel spirit isn't about sex distinctions. It's about an agenda of domination and destruc-tion. Satan doesn't care who does his dirty work, male or female. Whoever yields to his plan, he'll employ. Do you want some examples? Have you ever heard these words from the pulpit?

"If you ever leave this church, bad things will happen to you!"

"God called me to lead this church, and if you don't like it, get out!"

"What I do with my life is none of your business!"

"Around here, we're going to do things my way because God speaks through me!"

"We don't need a board to run the church. God calls men, not a committee!"

"Thus saith the Lord" (followed by a spiritual "trip to the woodshed" for the congregation).

"It's my way or the highway!"

"I lead, you follow—or get out of the way!"

You may be able to add to this list of Jezebel-inspired epithets hurled from the pulpit by domineering pastors. Now, get ready get ready for a really scary story.

I was ministering to a woman, whom we'll call Joy, who attended a large, very well-known church in America. If I were to mention the church and the pastor, everyone reading this book would know who it is. (Don't try to guess; I'm going to change a few non-crucial elements of this narrative to avoid speculation.) The demonized individual to whom I was ministering suffered from severe depression, many physical ailments, and a variety of torments that defied any medical or psychological relief. During the course of deliverance prayers a persona took over the individual's facial expressions and body language.

"Who are you?" I asked.

"I'm her pastor!" The demon then named this well-known, and highly esteemed Christian leader.

That probably got your attention. What was it I was experiencing? Some kind of demonic deception? A case of psychosis with the woman having taken on some mental projection of a separate identity?

No, Joy was experiencing what I have come to call (my coined definition) Dissociated Soul Transference (DST). I have written much on this topic and information is available from our offices and on our web site. Essentially, DST is an extreme form of a soul tie/bond. An individual becomes so closely connected to another, usually through a sexual or spiritual bond, that a dissociated part of the other's soul becomes embedded in the mind/soul of the victim. This usually happens implicitly, spontaneously. It can also be induced deliberately, a phenomenon well-known in some forms of witchcraft and black magic, in which case the injected soul-part is intentionally transmitted.

I once dealt with a woman from East Africa who had converted to Christ from a pagan, tribal culture. When she became a Christian, 25 different village witch doctors cursed her and tried to control her by each interjecting a soul portion into her mind. I actually spoke with each of the 25 shamans, and each gave a long, multi-syllable African name, which the woman told me was consistent with tribal names in her country. Each voice was distinctive in dialect and pronunciation. This phenomenon is quite common in tribal cultures but is little understood in the Western world. More important, getting each of these witch doctors to lift their curses led to the African woman being delivered.

Please note that I am not suggesting that the complete soul identity, the entire personhood of these evil shamans actually lived inside this African Christian woman; rather, what infested her was a very small portion of the shamans' souls, just the part connected to the curses they put on her. This phenomenon of an astral-projected soul part to attempt controlling another person's thinking is well-known in the darker realms of the occult.

This kind of at-a-distance mind control is also practiced by certain cults. Ever wonder how it is that some cult followers seem to lose their own identity and become a mere extension of their guru, even eventually acting and speaking like him/her? DST. How do reasonably intelligent people fall prey to Jim Jones kinds of leaders to the point of suicide? (For example the Hale Boop Comet Heaven's Gate cult of March 1997 that led 39 people to kill themselves? Each had a soul part of their leader, Marshall Applewhite, who at one time professed Christianity.) It's DST. Ever wonder how the late Rev. Moon could convince thousands of couples to marry at one time, in massive ceremonies, someone they had never met and had been chosen randomly by Moon himself? Each was required to take communion with wine that was said to contain a drop of Moon's blood. Now that's a *real* soul tie. DST.

Much more could be written about what I call Dissociated Soul Transference, which you can explore further at my web site (www.boblarson.org). But back to Joy's story. The voice that spoke to me claimed to be her pastor, or at least a soul portion of her pastor. I know much about this pastor, and I don't doubt that his accomplishments for the Lord have greatly furthered the Kingdom of Christ, for which I praise God according to Philippians 1:18 ("...in every way, whether in pretense or in truth, Christ is preached; and in this I rejoice..."). But—and make sure you get this—even a good and godly man of God can sometimes be deceived by a Jezebel spirit!

How can I say this? This particular pastor has been known to admonish his congregation, as some pastors unfortunately do, about the dangers of rejecting his church and leadership. He has warned of the consequences of opposing his spiritual stewardship. At times, he has even featured testimonies of people who once left his church. These individuals have told gut-wrenching accounts of all the misery they experienced while astray, only to have their problems solved when they returned to the fold. It is possible that some of these individuals were, indeed, walking in spiritual rebellion and there could be some credibility to some of their stories; but what happened, in my opinion, was an orchestrated agenda, perhaps even unintentional on this well-known pastor's behalf. (I'm giving him the benefit of the doubt here.) That plan was to maintain control over the congregation and keep the aggressive, ambitious aims of the church moving forward.

This particular pastor isn't the only one who has succumbed to this scheme of Jezebel; and I'm not saying that the pastor is demon-possessed. Like many American pastors, he has a success-driven, market-focused mentality where bigger is better and larger is spiritual. There is nothing wrong with that when at the core of the operating paradigm of the church is complete surrender and humility before Christ. Of special note, however, is the fact that this pastor has opposed the deliverance ministry. He doesn't believe Christians can have demons. By pointing this out I in no way want to detract from the personal sacrifices he has made, the hard work he has obviously engaged in, and his drive and zeal to reach people with the gospel of Christ.

But the facts are apparent. Either what I have described during Joy's ministry was some psychological aberration, a sham of Satan, or the real deal. I am telling it as it happened. I have known this woman for years and she has the highest integrity. She has no vendetta against this pastor and actually loves him and his ministry very much. Several other witnesses were present, including a successful pastor in active ministry. We all agreed to secrecy, never to reveal the particulars of what happened so that the reputation of this prominent pastor discussed here would ever be put in question by unscrupulous individuals. In fairness, this pastor has only done what many other pastors have done in their desperation to retain church members and keep the bills paid. Still, there can be no excuse for giving an open door to Jezebel.

What was the resolution to Joy's situation? I told this DST identity that he could no longer control the mind of this woman. I told the DST that he had no right to infringe upon the soul of another person, that the thoughts of man are the exclusive province of God (see Ps. 94:11). I told him to repent of what he'd done and that to the Lord alone he was held accountable.

"You must go back to your own mind and body, and never return to this woman again," I demanded.

That having been accomplished, I proceeded to cast out a religiously controlling spirit of Jezebel that inhabited Joy—infused there by her own pastor!

Don't miss the point. Jezebel can inhabit men. She can infest and influence even good men, otherwise godly men who walk with the Lord, except in their unsanctified desire for success and the need for manipulation and control to achieve that goal; and if Jezebel can do that then *all men*, especially spiritual leaders, need to pray daily that no presence of Jezebel ever influences their purposes and actions.

JEZEBEL ALIGNS WITH MANY OTHER DEMONS

The demon Lucifer (not *the* Lucifer but a designation of high rank in Satan's kingdom) often has Jezebel as a spiritual consort. They function as partners in spiritual crime. Their purposes are similar and they are cloaked in somewhat the same demonic demeanor of pride, arrogance, and opposition to all that is holy. They fit together, though Lucifer always has preeminence. Jezebel doesn't like taking second place to any spirit being, but Lucifer often pulls rank on her. They are loyal to each other as needs be. Often when the demon Jezebel is present, if the demonic bondage is particularly acute, Lucifer will lurk in the wings, hoping to hide behind Jezebel.

So does Mammon, one of the so-called "Seven Princes of Hell," as designated in occult literature. (More on this later.) Other demons commonly associated with Jezebel are Baal, Beelzebub, and Moloch. Baal (usually pronounced *bay*-uhl but more properly pronounced in the spirit world as *bah-uhl*) was variously worshiped as the god of thunderstorms, fertility, and agriculture. His name means "Lord" or "Master." In antiquity this demon deity took on various forms and functions, depending on the local characteristics assigned.

Baal's consorts included Ashtoreth and Astarte (the Aphrodite appellation came later with the Greeks), all forms of the same Lilith/Jezebel type. He was also worshiped as the sun god (Canaanites), a form I've also encountered during exorcisms. One of his transmutations was as Baal-Zebub, or as it is commonly referred to in Scripture "Beelzebub" (Lord of the Flies). Beelzebub was known in the New Testament as the "Prince of Demons" (such as in Matthew 10 and 12, Mark 3, and Luke 11). In antiquity Baal was also identified as Moloch (also Molech), though at times Moloch took on his own form. (Note: during deliverance sessions Moloch may act on his own or as another construct in conjunction with Baal.)

Baal/Moloch worship was condemned by Jeremiah (see Jer. 19:5) as being the god to whom apostate Jews sacrificed their children, as did the pagan cultures around them. All the forms of Baal were summed in the name Baalim, which means "many lords." Keep in mind that Baal and Ashtoreth were the chief deities worshiped by the Phoenicians, from whose kingdom Jezebel came to marry Ahab.

It was Samuel who stopped the worship of Baal (see 1 Sam. 7:4) but Solomon brought back the practice. Over and over Baal and Ashtoreth (also known as "Asherah," a reference to the worship of this deity in "the groves") were banished from Israel; for example in the time of Jehoshaphat and Hezekiah, only to be brought back to prominence when evil kings reigned, such as Ahaz. Manasseh tried to restore Baal worship to the prominence it held under Ahab (see 2 Kings 21:3). Only the judgment of Babylonian captivity finally purged all Israel of Baal's influence.

Perhaps one of the most important points here is that Jezebel seldom operates alone. She is either in tandem with the likes of Lucifer, as explained above, or in league with those who elicit direct worship such as Baal. Jezebel herself doesn't usually solicit devotion. She doesn't attempt to gain obeisance from her victims, just compliance. Her "thing" is obedience from the minions in her kingdom. She is the ultimate "control freak," requiring exacting performance from those demons associated with her. For practical purposes, those who minister deliverance need to know that, as with any den of vipers, where there is one, there are others. Where there is Jezebel, there are other powerful demons in accompaniment or association.

JEZEBEL ATTACKS ALL AGES

I've found Jezebel in children (though not often) and even the elderly (not as useful to the devil but a clever disguise). Just as I've pointed out that Jezebel is not gender pecific, neither is she age discriminatory. Once, an 82-year-old, godly grandmother swore a blue streak when Jezebel manifested. I've had young women with a Jezebel spirit scream in my face "F*** YOU!"—even when the host didn't speak English. I've had a child possessed with Jezebel spit in my face. Middle-aged women have suddenly turned seductive. An aging grandfather became violent when Jezebel manifested.

When one considers the attributes of Jezebel, which I've discussed at length, why should there be an age limit? Children can be controlling. Great-grandmothers can manipulate. Individuals at any age can exhibit arrogance. Beware the host of Jezebel who doesn't fit the stereotype: sensual, attractive, voluptuous, enticing. That elderly man or woman in the church can just as easily be a conduit for Jezebel's disruptions and chaos as an insubordinate teenager.

Now, don't be paranoid and see Jezebel everywhere, in every obstreperous person. Some individuals are just obnoxious. Some old folks are truly cantankerous. Some children are by nature stubborn and defiant. Such character faults can be changed by maturity and God's grace. But a Jezebel spirit never changes without deliverance. Its attitude expressed through a host of any age will always be directed toward disharmony and destruction of all that is good and godly.

JEZEBEL IS ASSOCIATED WITH WITCHCRAFT

The Jezebel of history introduced Israel to false, pagan worship of gods such as Baal. Her predecessor Lilith was the font of false worship and integral in generating the first lies of Eden. Wherever you find spiritualism, mediumship, New Age, psychic phenomena, Gaia worship, Wicca, and any form of demonic supernaturalism, you'll find Jezebel hard at work.

Where there is rebellion, there is witchcraft (see 1 Sam. 15:23). Where there is witchcraft there is Jezebel. But don't think exclusively of witchcraft in terms of bulbous-nosed crones with conical hats, bent over a boiling cauldron of newt's eye and frog's liver. It's not all about wands, spells, and dancing sky-clad (naked) around a midnight bonfire in a forest. Witchcraft can be a way of thinking, a way of acting, a method of religious subversion.

If it's deceptive and invasive of others' personal sanctity, it's witch-craft. If it subtly undermines legitimate authority in any realm (church, government, family) it's witchcraft. If it focuses on defying reasonable personal and societal moral boundaries, it's witchcraft. If it seduces godly beliefs, whether in the guise of humanism, secularism, atheism, agnosticism, it's witchcraft. Witchcraft is at the core of all rebellion against the rule and Word of God. And behind rebellion is almost always the spirit of Jezebel.

Jezebel is behind crystals, pyramid power, amulets, vision quests, pagan personal empowerment, "looking out for number one," yoga, psychics, channelers, Eastern meditation, Kundalini awakening, voo-doo, Santeria, spells, Harry Potter, vampires, shape-shifting...the list is almost endless. Yes, Jezebel is everywhere, everywhere there is non-Christian exploration of the supranatural and paranormal.

Jezebel is in the Ouija Board and the ads for fortune-tellers. Jezebel is in the appeal to experience unitary oneness with the universe, in the Buddhist call to mindless meditation, in radical Islam's beheading of those considered infidels, in every religious war ever falsely fought in the name of God. She's everywhere!

Everywhere—and nowhere that the saints of God stand up and fight her insidious assignments. Jezebel cannot abide the true presence of God. Jezebel can't tolerate surrendered obedience to the Word of God. Jezebel can't deceive those who are not ignorant of her devices. The purpose of this book, and your purpose after you've read it, is to make Jezebel *nowhere!*

Jezebel puts up a good act and might temporarily fool some, but the fruit of her intent will eventually be evident. Look for all the character-istics of this enemy as described in this book. Then you will recognize that her destruction, division, conceit, and lust for power are all around.

Chapter 14

JEZREEL'S DOGS, JEHU'S HORSE

"ALL GOOD THINGS MUST COME TO AN END." I'VE NEVER LIKED THAT old adage. It is negative and defeatist. It's based on fear, not faith. It's a lie not to be lived by Christians. In fact we who dwell in Christ are promised that, "He who has begun a good work in you will complete it until the day of Jesus Christ" (Phil. 1:6). It is rather more true that all *bad* things come to an end, an ignominious end. So says Proverbs 2:22—"The wicked will be cut off from the earth, and the unfaithful will be uprooted from it." A later proverb adds, "The labor of the righteous leads to life, the wages of the wicked to sin...the years of the wicked will be shortened (Prov. 10:16, 27).

SUMMARIZING JEZEBEL'S LIFE

When it comes to bad endings, welcome to the world of Jezebel! She started out as a princess, but ended up being pranced upon. Here's a recap of Jezebel's life as we've traced it in this book:

- Born in Phoenicia the daughter of Ethbaal, King of Tyre, to a life of privilege and worshiping her father's demon god Baal, of whom her father was a high priest. According to the Jewish historian Josephus, she was the great-aunt of the queen of Carthage.

- More as a diplomatic transaction than an act of love, she was married to King Ahab. He was the sovereign of the northern kingdom of Israel when it was divided into Israel in the north and Judah in the south.

- The pair turned Israel toward the worship of Jezebel's Phoenician deities Baal and his consort Asherah. Shrines and images were erected to these false gods. With 450 prophets of Baal she had brought with her from Phoenicia and 400 prophets of Asherah, she set about to establish her false gods as the preeminent deities to be worshiped in Israel. The 400 prophets of Asherah were so honored that they had a private, royal dining table in the palace, courtesy of Jezebel.

- Jezebel ordered the slaying of all the prophets of Jehovah and succeeded, except for Elijah and one hundred prophets, whom Obadiah (chief of King Ahab's household) hid, 50 each, in two caves.

- Elijah the prophet of Jehovah summoned all the prophets of Baal to a showdown on Mount Carmel to determine which God Israel would worship. His appeal has become a classic statement of spiritual fidelity: "How long will you falter between two opinions? If the Lord is God, follow him; but if Baal, follow him" (1 Kings 18:21).

- Despite all their energetic efforts (dancing, chanting, and cutting themselves) Baal's prophets were not able to call down fire from heaven. Then, even after Elijah had doused his sacrifice with water, fire fell and consumed both the sacrifice and the altar.

- Following this display of Yahweh's power and authenticity, Elijah took the prophets of Baal down to the Brook Kishon and had them executed. It is then that the lengthy drought in Israel was ended.

- Upon being informed by Ahab of what happened at Carmel, Jezebel pronounced a death sentence on Elijah, and in doing so brought a curse of death on her own head: "So let the gods do to me, and more also, if I do not make your life as the life of one of them [the slain prophets of Baal] by tomorrow about this time" (1 Kings 19:2).

- Elijah ran for his life into the wilderness and, overcome with suicidal depression, sat down under a broom tree. To preserve him from death, the Lord sent an angel with food and water.

- God directed Elijah to have his servant Elisha anoint Jehu, son of Nimshi, as king over Israel. The Lord reminded Elijah that He had kept 7,000 faithful followers who had not bowed to Baal.

- Ahab coveted the vineyard of Naboth and had him killed, by the designs of Jezebel. As a result Elijah told Ahab that he would be killed and that his entire royal house would be eradicated. At the same time the prophet declared Jezebel's eventual fate: "The dogs shall eat Jezebel by the wall of Jezreel" (1 Kings 21:23).

- Three years later, Ahab died in battle. His son Joram took over, but he was slain by Jehu and his body was thrown into Naboth's field (2 Kings 9:25).

- Ahab was killed by a random arrow that pierced a section of his armor. His body was brought to Samaria and buried there. The blood from his body that had soaked his royal chariot was licked up by dogs, near a pool where prostitutes bathed. After 16 years of reign, this was the end of the man whom Scripture says "did more to provoke the Lord God of Israel to anger than all the kings of Israel who were before him" (1 Kings 16:33).

With Ahab dead, the scene of action now switched to Jehu and Jezebel. The stage was set for the final demise of the wicked Jezebel. We know much about Jezebel, but who is this guy Jehu? Why does he so suddenly burst on the scene as the King of Israel—and the executioner of Jezebel?

Jehu as the Center of Action

In his youth Jehu had ridden behind Ahab as one of his guards. He was witness to the confiscation of Naboth's vineyard in Jezreel by false accusation and murder. With him at the time was Bidkar, a fellow comrade in Ahab's guard. Jehu was known for his aggressive, impulsive style. To this day, idiomatic language speaks of "driving like Jehu," referring to his driving his chariot "furiously" (the NIV says like "a maniac"), as described in Second Kings 9:20.

Elisha, the servant of Elijah, had anointed Jehu in secret as king over Israel. The prophet commissioned him to avenge the blood of Jehovah's prophets. Second Kings 9:6–10 records Elisha's directive to Jehu:

Thus says the Lord God of Israel: "I have anointed you king over the people of the Lord, over Israel. You shall strike down the house of Ahab your master, that I may avenge the blood of My servants the prophets, and the blood of all the servants of the Lord, at the hand of Jezebel. For the whole house of Ahab shall perish; and I will cut off from Ahab all the males in Israel, both bond and free. So I will make the house of Ahab like the house of Jeroboam the son of Nebat, and like the house of Baasha the son of Ahijah. The dogs shall eat Jezebel on the plot of ground at Jezreel, and there shall be none to bury her."

Jehu headed straight to Jezreel. On the way he encountered Ahab's son, King Joram. The king asked Jehu if he came in peace. Jehu replied, with his complete focus on his mission, "What peace, as long as the harlotries of your mother Jezebel and her witchcraft are so many?" (2 Kings 9:22).

Jehu promptly shot Joram with an arrow that entered between his arms and came out at his heart. In an act of vengeful irony, Jehu had the body of Joram thrown into the field of Naboth, the very vineyard that Ahab had seized by murder. After the killing of Joram, Jehu pursued King Ahaziah of Judah, who had conspired with Joram, and killed him too.

Next stop, Jezreel and Jezebel! Without any opposition Jehu entered the city of Jezreel, about 30 miles away. There was no resistance left. Jezebel was ready for Jehu. She knew he was coming. She put on her finest makeup and carefully arranged her hair. Whether she sought to seduce him or simply wanted to face her end with mock dignity, we can't be certain. She certainly hadn't lost her gift of sarcasm. "Have you come in peace...you murderer of your master?" (2 Kings 9:31, NIV)

Now that's the "pot calling the kettle black" if ever it was. What gall. She who slaughtered the prophets of God; she who instigated the murder of Naboth dares to accuse Jehu of such an impropriety? A murderer of the first rank accusing Jehu of the very crimes she had committed in copious bloodlust? That's Jezebel for you. Never at a loss for words and never losing her sneering wit. I've heard similar comments many times in hundreds of exorcisms:

"What's up with you? You're ugly!"

"Be careful, I spit."

"You think I'm bothered by the likes of you?"

"You try to feed me to the dogs, I'll feed you to the pigs."

"What's your God done for you lately?"

"I've been here for hundreds of years; what makes you think you can make me leave?"

Hubris to the max. Seldom at a loss for words. Harsh, biting remarks. Cynical irony. Grinning with demonic glee all the while. That's Jezebel.

Jehu was unfazed by the taunt of being called a murderer. His response was curt: "Who is on my side?" (2 Kings 9:32). At that point several eunuchs, likely part of the royal household of attendants, were faced with a decision: Would they be loyal to their evil queen, who had doubtless insulted and mistreated them countless times, or obedient to God's newly anointed ruler over Israel? Actually there wasn't much of a real choice. Ahab was dead and Jezebel's days were numbered. She was a faded queen, adorning herself one last time.

Jehu commanded the eunuchs: "Throw her down."

Throw her they did. As she tumbled from the window, her body was mutilated on the way and splattered the wall with blood. Even the horses of Jehu and his comrades were splashed with Jezebel's blood. Ignominiously, her already mangled body was trampled by the horses, and the dogs converged to lick her blood and gnaw at her flesh. When it was all over, those who came to bury her found only her skull, feet, and the palms of her hands. Even the dogs wouldn't eat those parts of her body.

What was left of Jezebel was scattered, as if it were manure, in a field. No burial, no mourning, no memorial. Jezebel was a queen, ruler over a vast realm, and yet there was never as much as a grave marker to recall her end. As for Jehu, he next commanded that all the royal princes of Ahab's household be hunted down and killed. The next day, the heads of 70 of them were piled in heaps outside the city gate. The entire family of Ahab and Jezebel had been eradicated.

What is to be learned, as practical lessons in dealing with Jezebel, from the actions of Jehu? He wasn't a faultless man. He was impetuous and a bit hasty, not exactly a thinking man's king. But he was decisive. When given an edict by the Lord, he acted upon the directive immediately.

LESSONS FROM THE SAGA OF JEZEBEL AND JEHU

- Jezebel is arrogant and defiant, down to the every end of her reign. I've seldom seen a demon so persistent, even when that evil spirit knows it is losing the battle for the host's soul. Battling Jezebel is a fight to the "bitter end." Jehu knew it would take total resolve to execute judgment on her. The same is still true today, when confronting this spiritual force of darkness.

- As a tactical device, when Jezebel refuses to comply with the exorcism process, I often call upon, in a spiritual sense, her devourers. My appeal is this: "Lord, send the dogs of Jezreel, now, to come and eat Jezebel's flesh and lick her blood!" In some instances, the demon of Jezebel will scream in torment, "No, not the dogs of Jezreel!" She often describe in words the horror of being spiritually consumed by "dogs," likely avenging angels who execute the Lord's judgment.

- In the face of Jezebel's overbearing pride and seeming self-confidence, Jehu is unflinching. During prayers of deliverance, and encountering this evil spirit any time, Jezebel is a master intimidator. She pushes every button; pulls out every insinuation; threatens with convincing terror; appeals to latent fears; looks for any weakness to exploit. She counts on her opponents to succumb to her taunts and mockery. She will seduce one moment and menace the next. She will poke inside your soul, looking for an opening, such as bringing up a former sin to make you feel unworthy. Whether facing Jezebel in an exorcism or confronting her in the circumstances of daily life, the warriors of God must be undeterred in pursuing the Lord's purposes.

- Jehu didn't allow Jezebel to bring up his past and question his motives. The Lord had commanded him to destroy all of Ahab's household, so the accusation that he was a murderer didn't faze him. Her comment does show how Jezebel will try to exploit an individual's weakest points, especially past hurts or failures. If her flattery doesn't get the job done, she'll try inducing a guilt trip of self-condemnation.

- Jehu didn't debate Jezebel's fate. There was no negotiation. No parley. If Jezebel is in your church, your home, or any situation you face, don't dialogue. There can be no transacting or debate about her end. Jezebel loves to ply her opponents with flattery and enticement while trying to avoid the action that is being taken against her.

- Jehu faced one evil woman, but we today face an entire culture infested with the spirit of Jezebel. This opposition from hell ranges from Madison Avenue advertising to Tinsel Town's erotic seduction on the big screen. In some ways every day is a battle with Jezebel, as she tries to get inside our minds. We must not be turned aside by all her enticements around us. Before you turn on that TV or go to that movie, remember that Jezebel may be there somewhere, waiting to dominate your mind.

- Jehu was a man's man. He was heroic, bold, and unaffected by Jezebel's painting of her face. In our world, I see far too many men who either succumb to this demon's sensual appeal or are willing to let her take over and run the show, especially in churches and marriages. In the home, or any romantic relationship, she'll use sex and affection, or the lack thereof, as a tactical means of control. If that doesn't work, she'll cleverly take over the leadership of the relationship. Unfortunately, some spiritually lazy men are only too willing to abdicate their responsibilities of biblical male covering and take the easy way out. They either don't want to confront Jezebel or they want what she offers in the bed, in social interaction, or in church affairs. Beware Jezebel's witchcraft!

SUMMING UP: JEHU VERSUS JEZEBEL

Jehu hated Jezebel! Look again at his reaction to her son Joram's attempt to ameliorate Jehu's rage: "What peace, as long as the harlotries of your mother Jezebel and her witchcraft are so many?"

Jehu was a conqueror, not a compromiser. His is the kind of spiritual leadership that is so needed today. Flashing through Jehu's mind must have been images of Jezebel's idolatrous altars to Baal, the bloody swords of those who killed the prophets of God, and the hedonistic orgies in the groves of Asherah. It had to stop!

The Christian world today all too often emulates the world's witchcraft. Too many churches are driven by market focus instead of Holy Ghost focus. Far too many pastors believe that Sunday morning's entertainment value and softly spoken words will keep the crowds coming. I may sound harsh, but take it from one who has seen the workings of Jezebel behind the curtain, backstage, thousands of times.

There must be no peace with the world's ways of winning souls. No peace with platitudes in the pulpit. No peace with out-of-order "words from the Lord." No peace with prophecies that don't come true. We must pull down the altars to Baal and oust the harlotries of Jezebel. When Joram wanted "peace," Jehu had but one answer: "What do you know about peace? Get behind me!" (2 Kings 9:18, TLB)

Wherever and whenever you are faced with Jezebel, be like Jehu. Be sharply defined in your spiritual intent. *Throw her down!*

Chapter 15

REPORTS FROM THE WAR FRONT

I HAVE BEEN PRIVILEGED TO HAVE A SPIRITUAL WEALTH OF experiences confronting the spirit of Jezebel. So, you can imagine, I've got lots of war stories to tell. I've woven a few of these accounts into previous chapters to illustrate particular points. There is so much to learn from these case studies in order to be more effective in spiritual warfare; consequently, I'm including some of my most memorable moments confronting Jezebel in this chapter.

Keep in mind these are not verbatim accounts. They are anecdotal summaries of what happened. The direct quotes are exactly as the words came forth from the demons. However, as in the accounts I have chronicled previously, the names and exact circumstances of the individuals involved have been changed to protect their privacy. Nothing has been done to change the facts of each report. For example, if the person receiving ministry was named Sarah, I may refer to her as Mary. I may change the gender if that doesn't interfere with the intent, such as relating what happened to a man as if it happened to a woman. My concern is that no specifics of my telling could compromise anyone's confidentiality if they wished that the specific facts of their encounter with me remain private. I may also alter the location or significant identifying factors. What I haven't changed are such things as the length of a curse, the name of the demon, the circumstances leading to the possession, or the actual flow of events.

Most important, I am citing exactly what the Jezebel demons said, as empirical evidence of their strategies and mindset. I once again remind the reader of certain critical facts which are vital to understand the process of encountering Jezebel spirits during deliverance:

GUIDELINES FOR DELIVERANCE NARRATIVES

- The name Jezebel (or Lilith, etc.) is a classification of certain evil spirits, according to that demon's particular function and individuated identity as established in the kingdom of darkness. There are many Jezebels at work, doing what that category of demon uniquely does.

- I interrogate demons, just as Christ did, to find out crucial information to successfully minister deliverance. I do not "dialogue" or "shoot the breeze" with demons in a casual or flippant manner.

- I test what the demons say by placing them under spiritual torment and threatening the judgment of God if they lie. I won't indicate having done this in each account, as doing so would be redundant in telling the stories. Demons can and do lie, but I have decades of experience in the tactical procedures necessary to prevent misinformation. Ministers of deliverance need to be sure that they are not operating on the basis of erroneous information forced from a demon.

- I do not place empirical information above Scripture. However, consider this. Many currently popular methods of soul-winning and church planting, and even church governance, are based on what has proven effective by observation. This is especially true when no clear biblical mandate is available to accomplish a particular goal, such as organizing church recovery groups.

- There are certain occasions when I do let a Jezebel demon speak more randomly or nonchalantly. It is rare, but when I feel led by the Holy Spirit to do so, I've given the demon enough leash to "hang itself" by exposing information after being too chatty. By doing this carefully I have gained valuable insights into demonic activity.

- These anecdotes aren't intended to establish doctrine or belief; rather, they are included to help devise counter-strategies. Demons have individuated states of being or personality, and categories of demons, such as Jezebel demons, tend to act similarly. If we know what those characteristics are, we can be more effective in setting people free from spiritual bondage. That is, after all, our supreme goal.

- If any reader has issues with my theological and practical approach to exorcism, my systematic theology and beliefs are thoroughly laid out in my 33 previous books, and especially in the courses of our International School of Exorcism, an online Bible college of spiritual warfare. Information is available by going to our web site (www.boblarson.org).

- When I cast out demons, there is a certain verbal protocol that I follow. That protocol is explained in our exorcism school. For brevity, I'll not repeat it each time I give the following accounts. The reader can assume that an exacting spiritual and verbal process was used to cast out the demons encountered in the stories below.

- Each account will feature, at the end of the story, the "takeaway," important lessons learned from these experiential observations.

DIANA OF THE EPHESIANS

It was your standard Christian Holy Land tour, including the seven church-cities of Revelation. Marlene and her husband were thrilled to take the trip of a lifetime, combining a vacation with redeeming spiritual value. They spent several weeks motoring and cruising through and around modern-day Turkey. Diana was particularly drawn to the city of Ephesus, near the present-day city of Izmir. I myself visited there one cold winter's day, after a flight from Istanbul, to walk the ancient, stone streets of this fabled city. My guide directed me to the magnificent ruins of the Library of Celsus and the theater where the Apostle Paul was confronted by an idolatrous mob who wanted to kill him (see Acts chapter 19).

But the most important place in Ephesus was the Temple of Artemis (Diana of the Romans) and earlier spiritual prototypes of Jezebel. In its time, this Temple was one of the Seven Wonders of the ancient world. It lies in ruins today, destroyed by the Goths in the third century, but also overcome by the conquering power of the gospel in Asia Minor. All that's left today are crumbled stones and pieces of the magnificent columns that once graced this mighty edifice. Nearby is a bookstore and small museum. Inside I saw a statue of Diana in the form of Aphrodite, the Greek goddess of fertility, her fecundity depicted by dozens of pendulous breasts hanging from her chest.

Our Christian friend Marlene saw all this too, but in the gift shop nearby she saw something else that caught her fancy: a silver pendant engraved with the image of Diana (aka, Jezebel!). She bought it and a year later attended one of our seminars with it hanging from her neck. I spotted it and called her to the front of the auditorium. I explained that by wearing this jewelry of a demonic deity that she could herself come under a curse. She accepted my admonition and agreed to renounce it; but when she tried to speak the words, "I renounce the pendant of Diana," the words wouldn't come from her mouth.

Then a demon spoke directly to me. "You're a joke. Who do you think you are? You're just a man." With that, the demon moved closer, making her body move seductively. "I like you. Perhaps we could get together sometime."

I held my cross and Bible directly in front of me. "I know you, Jezebel. We're not getting together anywhere, anytime, certainly not where you're going."

"Oh, you're no fun," Jezebel said, in mocking, sensual disappointment. "Like to know what I've done to this woman? She put on that pendant, and it gave us the right to torment her with a rare disease, and the doctors have no cure. That's not all. We have her four daughters as well."

Jezebel took control of Marlene's body and with her hands reached out to tug at the lapels of my suit coat. "Are you sure you don't like me?"

"I despise you," I responded, "and furthermore you're going to bow before me, a man, and a man of God."

Jezebel screamed hideously. "No! Never!"

More quickly than I could respond, Marlene's hands twisted into claw-like shapes and went straight for my throat. They clasped around my Adam's apple ready to rip my flesh and then stopped. Unseen angelic forces had taken over and prevented me from being choked.

"Lord, I ask for mighty angels to force this demon to its knees."

For a moment nothing happened. Marlene's body contorted in pain as it was physically obvious that something inside was violently resisting my command. Then, her body dropped, not just to her knees, but on all fours.

"Is Marlene's husband here?" I asked the audience.

A tall, lanky man stood and made his way to the stage. "What the demon said is true," he said. "The doctors tell us that Marlene can only eat twenty distinct foods. If she eats anything else, she'll die."

As he spoke Marlene haltingly stood up. I led her in a prayer of renunciation, breaking the curse of the Diana pendant and any other curses in her bloodline.

"So, Jezebel, do you have any more right to this woman?"

Pause. "I'm thinking. I'm thinking," Jezebel said in desperation.

"Obviously you don't, and you're going to come out now, in the Name of Jesus."

After a few minutes of intense spiritual struggle, Jezebel left and Marlene fell to the floor in relief and exhaustion. Then, suddenly she jumped to her feet and excitedly ran around the room. When she stopped, she said, "For months, since we returned from Ephesus, I've had severe pain in my stomach. Now, it's gone. It's gone!"

A year later, I returned to the city where I met Marlene. She and her entire family came to my seminar. An effervescent smile beamed from her face. When she saw me, she ran to me and hugged me. "I'm still free," she said as her husband and children stood at her side. "And guess what? I'm pregnant. The doctors said with all the physical problems I had that I'd never have any more children, but Jesus has healed me!"

The sight of that family of six, soon to be seven, encapsulates one of the reasons I am writing this book; and Marlene's story contains important information about Jezebel.

Takeaway from Diana of the Ephesians

1. Harboring, having in one's possession, a single occult artifact or object can open the door to demonization. This may not happen every time, but it's a risk not worth taking. Read again the story of Achan's sin in Joshua chapter seven. The wearing of the Diana pendant was a form of idolatry, even though that wasn't Marlene's intent.

2. As the maxim says, "Ignorance of the law is no excuse." Being unaware of spiritual dangers through ignorance

doesn't allow one to escape potential hazards. We are not to be ignorant of the devil's devices (see 2 Cor. 2:11).

3. Jezebel often brings with her other nasty demons. In Marlene's case, spirits of infirmity joined with Jezebel. The spiritual compromise of the pendant opened the door to extreme physical suffering.

4. Marlene's children were also affected by this curse of Diana. God has given spiritual authority to parents and entrusted them with the responsibility to provide their children with proper spiritual protection. Satan may use this principle in reverse and attack parental offspring when parents violate biblical boundaries.

5. Jezebel despises having to acknowledge legitimate masculine spiritual authority. This is why pastors and male Christian leaders are so often the target of Jezebel's schemes.

ISIS IN LOUISIANA

The man in front of me, named Mark, was receiving ministry for emotional healing when suddenly he started to rock back and forth. He raised his arms in slow, swaying gestures. Out of his mouth came a strange tongue. This exotic language was interspersed with wooing sounds, as he slowly blew breathe out of his body. His eyes were closed as if in some kind of trance. Something had taken over his entire being.

"I demand to know, in the Name of Jesus. What's going on and who is doing this."

The wooing sounds grew louder and more intense.

I insisted. "Tell me who you are!"

"I am Isis. These are the sounds of my priests of Karnak. This they do when they worship me. You're not supposed to hear this. This tongue is forbidden for the uninitiated to hear. Woo."

"Is Jezebel there with you?"

"Jezebel? Do not speak of her. She is below me. Before she was, I existed. I hate her. Loath her. She is beneath me. We compete for the same worship, but I've been here more than 3,000 years."

"And how were you worshiped?"

"Pornography. Orgies. Perversion. Have you not seen my images on my temples?"

Actually, I had. I'd been to the Valley of the Kings in Egypt several times. Anyone who goes to this ancient site in Upper Egypt, near the present city of Luxor about 300 miles south of Cairo, will also see a myriad of wall frescos depicting the religion of ancient Egyptian dynasties. Here I've visited the temple complexes at Karnak and the Valley of the Kings and Valley of the Queens.

Many of the columns of Karnak still stand, carved with thousands of images of worship and the recounting of battles. Walking among these imposing structures, which once supported a luxuriously painted ceiling 40-plus feet above, must have been awe-inspiring. As this demon Isis spoke, I could image the priest of Isis with their swaying censers solemnly walking the colonnaded corridors of Karnak. To the people of that time, it must have seemed otherworldly.

But it was in the Valley of the Kings and Queens that I saw the true essence of the sophisticated but debased worship of Isis, especially at a necropolis where is found the rock-cut tomb of Nefertari. Inside, preserved by the dry climate and millennia of inaccessibility, are the polychrome reliefs untouched by tomb raiders. Because of my involvement in spiritual warfare, I knew what to look for; the things that the tour guides would be too embarrassed to show to the average tourist.

"Show me the images of Hathor," I said to my guide. He looked at me astonished. He shook his finger "No."

I insisted. There was no use trying to explain who I was and what I did, and thus why I'd be interested in researching ancient Egyptian religious pornography.

The guide motioned hesitantly, almost secretively, and crept toward a less-illuminated, further reach of the tomb. His eyes darted as if he were afraid someone was watching. It was obvious he didn't want to take me there, but I wasn't going to be deterred. I insisted that he proceed until he finally motioned for me to follow.

Finally, in a darkened section of the tomb he lit a match that seemed to light up the entire inner chamber. He pointed toward a wall adorned with colors as brilliant as the day they were applied 3,300 years ago. The wall glowed with the usual depictions of the ancient Egyptian deities and demigods, all demons I had met one time or another while ministering exorcism: Osiris, god of the underworld, green-skinned and sporting a pharaoh's beard along with his traditional crook and flail, the incestuous brother of Isis; Horus (known for his ubiquitous eye of Wedjat or Ra symbol), killed by his brother Set (Lucifer to the ancient Egyptians) and brought back to life by Isis by means of a spell cast over replica of genitalia.

The guide beckoned for me to go yet deeper into the tomb. Here he pointed to Hathor, consort of Ra and Horus, believed in some legends to be the mother of Horus. I cringed at what I saw, the most explicit of details not fit to recite. This goddess of sex and fertility was depicted as a cow, suckling humans. All around her, and Isis, were humans and animals in various stages of bestiality. This background is important to know; the evil depravity of Isis/Hathor/Jezebel predates that of the Phoenician princess.

Back to the ministry time. What made this exorcism of Mark most interesting is that this demon goddess Isis was inside a *male*. Why? I wanted to know and asked.

"Pornography. This man and his father were obsessed with it, just like so many men today. You know, we're slowly taking over the mind of America," Isis cackled. "Just like it was in my days of glory in Egypt."

"But how did you, Isis, specifically get from Egypt to this man?"

"Well, if he hadn't looked at pornography the door wouldn't have been open. But it was really the house that gave us the right."

"What house?"

"The one he lived in down south. Ask him."

I bound Isis and asked Mark if he'd ever lived anywhere in the south.

"Louisiana," he replied. "It was a remodeled old plantation-style house. I always felt strange living there, like something was watching me all the time. That's about the time I personally got into porn, especially on the Internet."

Back to Isis. "So what's the house got to do with your possessing this man?"

"There was a curse on the house. One of the contractors during the remodeling phase tried to seduce the owner's wife. She said no and he vowed revenge. There's a lot of voodoo down there, you know," Isis smirked.

From Egypt more than 3,000 years ago to a home in Louisiana to my office in Arizona. What an evil journey; but it ended that day once Mark's sins were dealt with and the curse from the Louisiana home was broken.

Takeaway From Isis in Louisiana

1. Ancient evil can morph from one culture to another, one country to another, over great expanses of time. Because demons like Jezebel operate on the basis of certain evil principles, wherever those principles are in play, these evil spirits can torment.

2. One doesn't have to worship a demon to get a demon. All that's needed is to participate in some sin that is connected to the character of that particular demon. Mark's sin was pornography. He wanted sexual stimulation, but what he got was a terrible evil from long ago.

3. Jezebel has many forms, both before and after her incarnation as the wife of Ahab. We call this demon Jezebel as a popular-usage designation, but it may be encountered in other forms.

4. It's helpful when doing deliverance to have at least a general working knowledge of ancient evil structures of Satan's kingdom.

5. Jezebel can operate through multiple open doors and curses. In this case, since Jezebel/Isis are associated with witchcraft, Mark's unknowingly falling victim to a voodoo curse made matters worse. It might be argued that this wasn't fair spiritually. Of course, first of all, nothing is fair in Satan's kingdom. Second, anytime an individual who is a Christian rents, owns, or otherwise occupies a dwelling a cleansing of that place should be done before habitation. Because I travel considerably I even pray over each hotel room that I enter. Never take the risk of picking up a spiritual contagion by occupying a particular space.

THE WHORE OF THE NEPHILIM

"We are the Nephilim, and we'll be back. We almost corrupted all mankind before, and we haven't given up our goal. You wait. You watch. We are the sons of god and we will return!"

Demons say outrageous things. They boast, lie, and exaggerate. ("I'm legion," is a common claim.) They mislead. But sometimes they are dead serious about their intent; not just what they intend to do with their victim, the host they possess, but larger goals that embrace eschatology and prophecy. And demons who claim to be part of the Nephilim have decidedly very ambitious purposes.

Genesis chapter 6, in the first seven verses, speaks of this ancient phenomenon. The Bible refers to Nephilim in various ways: "heroes of old" (Gen. 6:4, NIV), "men of renown" (Gen. 6:4), "sons of god" (Gen. 6:2). Most Bible scholars believe that their evil was one reason for the worldwide devastation of the flood. All humans, except Noah and his household, were so corrupted with demon-human, hybrid genetic pollution that nothing less than extinction would eradicate this extreme evil.

The word "Nephilim" is variously translated as "fallen" and as "giants." These were the beings Caleb and Joshua spied upon in the land of Canaan. The faithless spies, who opposed the good report of Caleb and Joshua, said of the inhabitants, "We saw the giants" (Num. 13:33). "We saw the Nephilim," says the same verse in the NIV.

Church fathers of the first three centuries believed that the Nephilim were a mongrelized race which came from the insemination of female humans by a specific class of fallen angels, which were demons. (They are also known as "the Watchers.") Later theologians took such references to mean that the "sons of God" were from the godly line of Seth, and the "daughters of men" were ungodly offspring of Cain. Adding some confusion to this narrative is the fact that after the flood there were still giants, though only for a period of time (see Gen. 6:4).

There are several other references to giants, such as the descendants of one Anak and Arba, father of Anak. Og (from which we get "ogre") had a bed almost 15 feet long, and was said to be the last "remnant of the giants" (Deut. 3:11). One thing is certain from Bible history: there was a race of beings at least twice the size of humans as we know them, and there must have been some kind of demonic-human cohabitation before, and shortly after the Flood. These giants were totally evil and never followed the ways of Jehovah and are always associated with depravity, such as that leading to the Deluge. (The noncanonical Book of Enoch speaks at length of the Nephilim.)

Some theologians, especially those not favorably disposed to spiritual warfare, argue against the idea of superhuman beings as the offspring of demons having sexual intercourse with human females. Such comingling would not be possible, they argue, since demons are spirit, not physical, and thus could not have reproductive capabilities; however, the book of Jude, verses 6 and 7, speaks of "angels who did not keep their proper domain" (translated "first estate" in the King James) and have since suffered an unusual judgment of being bound by "everlasting chains." Their sin? "Going after strange flesh" (Jude 7, KJV).

In reality, we don't know whether or not demons are incapable of insemination of humans. After all, some unusual genetic mutation must have given way to gigantic offspring, giants and a super race. All ancient mythologies are filled with tales of such beings which often cohabited with humans. Heathen scholars taught this in the eras before Christ. Jewish theologians accepted the idea.

Remember that demons retain some of their angelic-like qualities before the fall, and we know that good angels could appear as humans and even ate food. In other words, their assumed bodies did in some way relate to the physical world in which they appeared. Spirit and matter do seem to have some interchangeability, no matter what later Christian scholars taught.

If such paternity was possible after the Flood as well as before, how can its possibility be dismissed completely in our age? If theoretically possible, this would not be the only time that St. Augustine, John Chrysostom, and John Calvin were wrong. After all, esteemed Christian leaders such as Calvin were not especially favorable toward a worldview of spiritual warfare.

Supposing that the Nephilim were the hybrid progeny resulting from some kind of sexual conjugation, what does that mean to our study of Jezebel? The same demons who spoke to me of their aims to genetically pollute mankind (as referenced at the start of this particular narrative) didn't stop with the simple quote above.

"We will be back," they boasted. "We were the master race before, and through the Antichrist we will be again!"

As I faced these boastful demons, my face betrayed my skepticism. The demons retorted, "How do you think the pyramids were built? How do you think that monuments of old were possible without the aid of modern implements? We did it. It was easy for us. You humans are so stupid. You don't know what we can do and how we operate at a genetic and even a molecular level in the code of life."

All this was said in the midst of an exorcism of Jezebel. The spirits speaking to me claimed to have come down from the second heaven and intended to do what those in the "chains of darkness" could not do now.

"We will rule! We will bring back Babylon! You think you're so smart today. The kingdoms of the past weren't built by normal intelligence. They did it through divination, and that's how we'll do it again. That harlot Jezebel will make it all possible."

I repeat the principle I stated earlier, that we don't build doctrine upon demonic utterances. But where the Bible is not explicit, and when what evil spirits say fits into the design of Satan as described in the Bible, such information about the specifics of how remarkable evil will be achieved can give important insights. And one of those insights is that Jezebel, the whore of the Nephilim, is an important part of Satan's end-times plan.

Takeaway From the Whore of the Nephilim

1. Factoring in the concept of demon-human cohabitation can explain a lot of unanswered questions about ancient history, if we conclude that the spawn of evil resulted in a superhuman race of beings with strength and intelligence far beyond mere humans.

2. The concept of Nephilim helps to also explain why there seems to be such an increase in the phenomenon of incubus/succubus/spiritual mates. Though apparently not yet currently able to genetically produce hybrid children, evil spirits with this assignment may be making a trial run of their ultimate intentions.

3. That sexual sin is at the core of all demonic corruption explains why there is such an obsession with aberrant sexuality in our age. The destruction of biblical

boundaries of human sexuality is an achievement that is necessary before the "falling away" spoken of in Second Thessalonians 2:3 takes place and the "son of perdition" is revealed.

4. Jezebel foments the circumstances and conditions the times for this great apostasy of the times of Last Days' tribulation. Revelation 2:20, which we've discussed before, illustrates that Jezebel will corrupt the people of God with sexual immorality, including forms of demonic-human cohabitation.

5. The Nephilim of our time are ruling spirits from higher realms who have been held in reserve by the devil, awaiting the times at hand. Just as the Jezebel of Elijah's time corrupted true religion, the Jezebel of the coming Apocalypse is even now corrupting humanity through abnormal sexuality. (Of note, some commentators of Scripture believe that the rebuke to Thyatira's Jezebel was directed at an actual bishop's wife who claimed to be a great teacher and instead used her sexual prowess to seduce the people of God into sinning.)

JEZEBEL AS MEDUSA

"El canti, calia senti. Un sebo, asti lenti. This one is mine and so are her children!"

The strange words, some kind of demonic tongue, meant nothing to me. Neither did the boast. But I recognized the arrogance.

"By what right do you claim this woman and her children?"

"I get tired of talking to you every time I turn around," Jezebel responded. "Brian said I could have her three children."

"Brian?"

"Her cyber-lover. She hasn't told you about him?"

I commanded the demon to be silent, stop manifesting, and I called back to consciousness the woman, Linda, a thirtyish, divorced, single parent of three young girls. She had arranged to privately see me as part of our Personal Spiritual Encounter outreach.

"Who's Brian? You haven't mentioned him before. Is he someone you met online? He claims some kind of right to your children."

Linda dropped her head slightly as if in shame. "Yes, I met him on a chat site for singles. He seemed like a nice guy, so I told him about my family."

"But you know nothing about this guy," I remonstrated. "What did he want?"

"Cybersex. As I Christian, I went along. I figured since it wasn't real sex that it would be okay. In fact when I was in my deepest depression, he talked me out of killing myself. I was so grateful I went along with his..." Linda paused for a moment. "You know, his requests."

"Requests?"

Linda began to weep. "For sex. Just online, just words on a computer screen. We weren't really doing anything."

I looked at her skeptically. "That's how you justified what you were doing?"

"Yes, until..." This pause was longer. "Until he talked about having sex with his daughter and asked if he could do it with one of my girls."

I shook my head in disbelief at such transparent lack of parental caution.

Linda burst forth into heavy sobs. "I know it was wrong, but I was so lonely. When I told Brian 'No,' that's when he told me he was a powerful witch and would do it anyway, over the Internet. I didn't think he was serious until my oldest daughter starting having nightmares about some man coming into her room at night."

In an instant the demons inside Linda took over and lunged toward me. My chair went backward, and I did a full reverse somersault, ending up on my back with her on top of me, struggling to strangle me. Only an alert response from several prayer intercessors who were helping me prevented serious injury.

As my rescuers pulled Linda away, the demons screaming profanities and threats, I quickly regained composure and rebuked the evil spirits for daring to attack me.

"I call judgment from God upon you for assaulting the man of God," I yelled, defiantly thrusting my Cross of Deliverance toward the demons. "Go down; get out of the way so I can talk to Linda."

As Linda came to herself she was horrified to see me on the floor recovering from the attack. "What happened? What's going on?"

We explained to her that it was her demons, not her who knocked me over. After a few minutes of calming her, we continued.

"Don't you see?" I told Linda. "This guy Brian is a pedophile. He was trolling for victims. He was setting you up to molest one of your daughters. And you gave the demon Jezebel the right to attack you and your children."

"I understand that now," the terrified woman replied. "What's this Jezebel look like? After the incident with Brian I started having nightmares of a hideous woman with a head full of snakes, like her hair was full of them."

"Medusa," I answered, "the ancient Greek goddess who was supposed to have poisonous snakes writhing in place of her hair. She was supposed to be beautiful but terrifying. The water god Poseidon raped her in the temple of Athena. The goddess Athena was so angry that she turned Medusa's beautiful hair into serpents. So the legend goes, any man who looks at her turns to stone."

I paused and looked intensely into Linda's eyes, peering right into her soul. Medusa knew what I was doing.

"All right, all right, so you've found me!"

"And exactly, who are you?"

"Medusa; you just described me." A sickening grin crossed Linda's face. "Want to see my snakes?" the demon said seductively.

"I want your real name," I shot back in a demanding tone.

The demon rolled its eyes in mock disgust. "Rape, Molestation, Pornography, Incubus! How many names do you want?"

"Like I said, your real name. Sure, you're all of this. But we both know who you are. Jezebel!"

Linda was a small woman, I suspected barely 100 pounds. The four people accompanying me held on to her as tightly as possible and could barely restrain her. Supernatural strength surged through her body. She spat, cursed, and struggled to get free.

"One hundred generations, that's how long we've been here. Her ancestors offered blood to us to get sex, and we're not leaving now. She hasn't even told you about all her other Internet sex. Like the time she chatted with a woman, pretending to be a man. That time I got into her as Ishtar. Want to know her Twitter and Facebook name? 'Golden girl Ishtar.' Creative, don't you think."

Once more I forced the demons to withdraw temporarily and called back Linda. She confessed to using a variety of social media names, at least a dozen, to communicate with all kinds of individuals of both sexes. I had her list then all out, and one by one we renounced them, also breaking the soul ties with every person with whom she had sexually communicated online.

Linda also confessed to assuming at least ten identities: gay male, female prostitute, bored housewife, teenage virgin, and others. Her assumed personae were borrowed from Japanese Anime (hand-drawn or computer-generated animations, usually featuring oversized eyes and emphasizing quick action and over-dramatized themes) and various mythologies. From her smartphone, she showed me various poses she sometimes used, ranging from baby-doll costumes to Elvira-like witchiness. It took hours to work through all her cyber personalities.

Each one was renounced; at the same time, various demonic variations of Jezebel manifested and had to be laboriously confronted, bound, and prepared for judgment. Some demons had been transferred by the soul bonds she had made through online sexual conversations. Others entered as she had role-played and become all too literally the identity she was mimicking.

Many hours later, with a long list of demons and cyber-identities in hand, I bound all the demons and fake personalities as one under Medusa and Jezebel. The expulsion of these demons in all their variations was violent and vocal. They came out progressively in layers, like peeling back an onion. In the end, Linda collapsed in total exhaustion from the ordeal.

The purpose of this narrative is to serve as a Web-age warning to anyone who thinks that taking on fake, morally inappropriate roles during online communication isn't "real" sin. Remember, Christ warned in Matthew 5:28 that to look with lustful intentions is to commit the deed already in the heart. This is true whether frequenting porn sites or indulging in salacious conversations. These are areas that Jezebel exploits, and she is eager to engage in computer-age evil, which has made conjurations feasible digitally.

Takeaway from Jezebel as Medusa

1. Evil imaginations (see 2 Cor. 10:3–5) can be as damaging to the soul as actual acts of evil done in the flesh. Speaking forth sin can be as much an open door to the devil as doing sin.

2. As we've established many times in this book, Jezebel wears whatever disguise suits her purposes of the moment. She is a transformational spirit who takes on many ways of appearing, including both historical and contemporary modalities; but all these deceptions have the same intent, to control and manipulate and to maximize her destructive purposes.

3. Jezebel is creative and inventive. Masses of people no longer indulge in temple prostitution and offer their offspring as sacrifices to idols; yet, in a figurative way, this is what Linda did. She indulged in a form of cyber-prostitution. She used the clicks on a computer keyboard and mouse to communicate her desires and sexual availability. Along the way she nearly offered her own child as a sexual sacrifice to a man in cyberspace she had never met or seen; a connection that could have ended up in actual molestation.

4. Medusa was one of many alternative identities that Jezebel assumed. Each variation manipulated a difference aspect of Linda's consciousness. The totality of Jezebel's deception created a multifaceted attack.

5. Not only do children need to be monitored for Internet activity, but adults also need to be self-censoring about what they do online. The computer age presents marvelous opportunities for communicating faith and values. It also can be a trap for the undiscerning adult who gets sucked into its worldwide web of evil.

WHAT THESE NARRATIVES TEACH US

There are many lessons to be learned from these accounts, and there isn't enough room in this book to contain everything of which we need to be aware. Each narrative represents an encapsulated example of what could be hundreds and hundreds of stories I might tell; yet these few examples of Jezebel's wiles should give the reader a heightened awareness of how inventive and corrupt this demon's capacity for total intemperance can be. Jezebel's adjustability of evil, the art of shifting from one form of wickedness to another, is almost limitless. Only by complete dependence of God's power and wisdom can we hope to conquer this #1 enemy of all humanity.

Chapter 16

BEHIND THE SKIRTS
OF JEZEBEL

THOSE WHO KNOW ME WELL UNDERSTAND THAT I AM PRIMARILY AN objectivist, a researcher with a forensic mind. Frankly, I cringe at the way that some wide-eyed, gullible Christians are so ready to believe what every preacher and self-proclaimed prophet says is a message from the Lord. I don't discount the reality of revelation and contemporary interventions by God, but in my view these supernatural insights happen far less often than is claimed, and with far less specificity than purported. So when I say that the Lord has given me a "new revelation," the reader can be certain that a lot of thoughtful prayer and critical analysis has gone into that conclusion. I am so much fact centered that the Lord really has to write large what He wants me to see if it's outside the box of my normal thinking patterns.

Yes, I am an exorcist, and that very calling means that I regularly operate in a supernatural environment. When confronting demons, words of knowledge and wisdom are often needed to circumvent the constant deception of demons; but even then I am careful to focus mainly on observable facts and employ supernatural understanding only when it's necessary. I thus avoid the trap of some deliverance ministers who operate too subjectively, who are too suggestible and easily influenced by the perfidy of evil spirits.

I say all of this to underscore that the account I am about to share is very unusual. The following is one of those rare instances in my life and ministry when the Lord truly got my attention in a supernatural way. I received a new revelation.

THREE DAYS, THREE EXORCISMS, GOD SPOKE

I was in Ukraine. As of the time of the writing of this book, I've been there, and to Russia and Eastern Europe, eight times in the past four years. Once each year I am a visiting professor of spiritual warfare at the largest Bible college in Eastern Europe. Once a year I also return to teach at the local campus of our International School of Exorcism. It was during such a visit that this new revelation came to pass.

As a minister of deliverance one might say that I've seen it all. I've encountered nearly every kind of evil force, witnessed the most unthinkable instances of human suffering, and faced the most insidious of supernatural entities. But something was very different for three unique days in Ukraine. My epiphany took place during the height of tensions created by warfare in the Eastern part of the country, immediately following the shooting down of Malaysian Airlines flight MH17 and the senseless killing of nearly 300 passengers.

Less than 100 miles from where the plane was shot down and the fiercest fighting was taking place, I was fighting an unusual spiritual war. Three days in a row, during three extremely violent and intriguing exorcisms, I faced the same demon in three different people. These confrontations resulted in pulling back the curtain that was hiding an evil I had only brushed up against before. This time, it faced me with all its fury.

Anastasia, a Troubled Drug Addict

Anastasia was a 25-year-old young woman with a lifetime of pain on her shoulders. Her beautiful face and relaxed smile hid torment that most will never suffer in an entire lifetime. As I taught the students of our School of Exorcism she sat on the front row, assenting often to important points that I conveyed through my Russian translator. But when it came time to pray for those suffering spiritual oppression, she quickly changed—her "Amens" turned to deep-throated growls. Her smile turned to snarling disdain. As I approached her, she lunged for me and had to be restrained.

Anastasia's left forearm was covered with lateral streaks of scar tissue, where she had inflicted suicidal slashes with knives and razors. Her right arm displayed a large mass of seared flesh where a drug injection once led to a life-threatening infection. She had been a prostitute, a (self-) cutter since age 15, addicted to drugs since a teen, repeatedly beaten by her mother. Her earliest years were spent under Communism in Soviet Russia, when life was hard and many turned to alcohol and drugs to cope. She had since become a Christian and was intent on learning as much as possible about spiritual warfare.

The exorcism process revealed a three-generation curse going back to female ancestors in Russia who were raped and murdered by the Soviets because they were Christians. Naturally I realized then that Jezebel was present, along with spirits of Rape and Death. Her deliverance was extremely physical and required several strong men to restrain her from causing harm.

At one point, her demons spoke English and cursed me with coarse, American obscenities, which was a shock to those who knew Anastasia personally. She spoke no languages other than her native tongue, Russian; she certainly didn't know how to communicate in English. In fact, I finished the final part of the exorcism in English with the demons consenting to their doom. They spoke and understood every word.

Identifying that Anastasia was possessed by spirits of Death, Murder, Suicide, and Jezebel were easy conclusions, based on her life's circumstances. But the most dominant demon was a surprise. It wasn't until I was almost ready to expel Jezebel and her kingdom that an even more powerful demonic force surfaced to fight against me. This hideous fallen angel had been hiding behind Jezebel. He was there because Anastasia's ancestors had worshiped this god with the blood sacrifice of infants.

Marina, Woman of Many Marriages

The next day, as I again ministered to students of the School of Exorcism, God drew my attention to a 41-year-old mother of two. Marina was attractive, well-spoken, and enthusiastic about learning to minister deliverance. I learned that, like the woman at the well in John 4, she had been married four times in her short lifetime. Naturally, I suspected the presence of my #1 demonic enemy and, when I began praying with Marina, Jezebel quickly manifested. As also might be expected, Lilith was present. As with Anastasia, Marina's ancestors had performed blood sacrifices of infants many generations ago. Also like Anastasia, Marina's demons addressed me partially in English, a language unknown to her.

After more than an hour of battling Marina's demons of Lilith, Death, and Jezebel, I was ready to initiate my protocol of demonic expulsion, described earlier in the book; but just before I pronounced the judgment of God on these evil spirits, I felt a spiritual hesitation compelling me to stop in mid process. As with Marina, I sensed that Jezebel was hiding an even more powerful spirit than she. I demanded to know what demon was behind the Jezebelian orchestration of Marina's lifelong, relational misery. Then it happened. Raging forth from within this otherwise composed and pleasant woman was the same fierce evil spirit that had tormented Anastasia. This demon was cast out, but not without a tough battle that overcame Jezebel's considerable fighting skills.

Anton in Energodar

The next day I traveled to the city of Energodar, Ukraine, famed as the location of the largest nuclear power plant in Europe, which supplies electricity to places as far away as Portugal. The auditorium where our meeting was to be held, the largest in the city, was jammed. A standing-room-only crowd of nearly 1,000 people was desperate to experience the power of Christ. After my teaching on spiritual warfare, I walked through the audience, my Bible and Cross of Deliverance in hand. I was seeking those to whom the Holy Spirit would lead me for prayer.

As I made my way up and down the aisles of the jam-packed room, scores of people manifested demonic states. Some wept hysterically. Others shook with spasms of torment. Screams and wails of grief filled the room. I could have chosen any one of them for direct, one-on-one ministry; but I hesitated, feeling that there was someone among the masses destined for an encounter with Christ. Someone that, if I were patient, God would reveal to me.

Then I spotted that person. It was a young man sitting inconspicuously toward the back of the room. He was quietly slouched in his seat, almost as if he were trying to hide. Our eyes locked for a micro-second, long enough for me to see the hatred and evil in his eyes—the look of Jezebel. Through my Russian interpreter, I asked the man to make his way toward a side aisle so that I could pray for him. He did so hesitantly. The moment I touched his forehead with holy anointing oil, he reacted violently, and I narrowly avoided injury. It took seven men to get him under control and quite literally drag him to the stage. There, the entire audience could observe the exorcism process.

His name was Anton, and he had come to the meeting with some friends who, like him, were in drug rehab. Anton declared that his addiction was alcohol. When I asked if he were a Christian, he replied, "Nyet" ("No" in Russian). So, before attempting to deal directly with any demons, I led him in a prayer of repentance and confession of sin. As he prayed the "sinner's prayer" his eyes darted back and forth wildly. Something inside him was angry and terrified at what was happening.

At one point, as the demons struggled against the human restraint of the strong men who assisted me, I prayed that the Lord's judgment would fall to weaken these evil spirits. I shouted, "In the Name of Jesus, be smitten with divine vengeance!" The entire auditorium went pitch black for the space of about 30 seconds, though it seemed much longer. Considering the physical violence that preceded the prevailing darkness, one could sense the tension of the audience. After witnessing the violent struggle for Anton's freedom, undoubtedly no one was shocked by this unusual occurrence at such a critical juncture during the exorcism.

When lights suddenly came back on, the exorcism process resumed. The demon of Addiction revealed a multi-generational curse rooted in the ancient blood sacrifice of children—just as in the cases of Anastasia and Marina. I demanded to know the name of the Strong Man, the main demon behind the bondage of alcoholism and Jezebel. To my astonishment, it was the same demon I had battled for two successive days.

Anastasia, Marina, Anton—What's Going On?

Three days, three exorcisms. Each deliverance had a slightly different dynamic of spiritual enslavement. Anastasia: sexual abuse and self-injury. Marina: dysfunctional and broken relationships. Anton: severe alcohol addiction. Each had the spirit of Jezebel. And each was a victim of ancient curses invoked by the blood sacrifice of infants.

That's not all. Despite their different spiritual dynamics, at the root of all their evil was the same Strong Man, a powerful ruling evil spirit, one of the so-called Seven Princes of Hell in classical Satanism. In each case this evil being hid behind Jezebel. Was this all just an interesting coincidence, a serendipitous confluence of circumstances that I just happened to encounter three days in a row? My spiritual hunch was, "not likely."

I had to know if there was some deeper spiritual truth that God was revealing to me. I returned to my hotel room and stayed up all night in prayer, study, and contemplation. Gradually, in the wee hours of the morning the Holy Spirit congealed all that had happened in the past 72-plus hours into a new revelation.

The demon that possessed all three, Anastasia, Marina, and Anton, wasn't unknown to me. We had met before during deliverance, though certainly not in three people, three days in a row. What was the Lord showing me? Had this demon been hiding under my nose for years, concealed by Jezebel, his spokesperson and shield? Was this one reason I so often encountered Jezebel? Was she there to protect the spiritual territory ruled by this extremely powerful demon?

Like an unfolding mystery of iniquity, the evidence compounded.

Seven Deadly Sins and Seven Abominations

This ruling spirit is embodied by one of the historical seven deadly sins recognized by the Church, particularly developed in religious thought by the fourth-century monk Evagrius Ponticus. (Pope Gregory I codified this list in the sixth century and it was employed by Dante in the composition of his *Divine Comedy*.) These sins have been viewed in Christianity as unique because they are the origins of all other sins. Identified in the early Church, these seven sins were widely recognized through artistic depictions that imposed them upon the collective consciousness of the masses.

In the Bible, the sixth chapter of Proverbs lists seven evils which are detestable to God:

> *These six things the Lord hates,*
> *Yes, seven are an abomination to Him:*
> *A proud look,*
> *A lying tongue,*
> *Hands that shed innocent blood,*
> *A heart that devises wicked plans,*
> *Feet that are swift in running to evil,*
> *A false witness who speaks lies,*
> *And one who sows discord among brethren* (Proverbs 6:16-19).

Though not as precise as the seven deadly sins and more defined by action than condition, this series of sins embodies the actions of all Seven Princes of Hell, but more particularly the demon of which I write, the one covertly hidden by Jezebel.

What this Demon Does

As I sought the Lord during that long night of spiritual searching, it became more and more clear what this demon does. My fingers flew over my laptop as I listed all the ways this one is embedded in the evil of our world. This demon is at the root of the following:

- Wars and international conflicts

- Crime, violence, and murder

- Pornography and prostitution

- Marital strife and divorce

- Failure and ruination in many areas of life

- Sickness and disease that destroys not only the body but all livelihood and occupation

That's quite a list to attribute to one evil spirit; but remember, this demon operates at the foundational level of all human wickedness and evil intentions.

THE IDENTITY OF DEMONS

The Bible says far more about demons than most Christians realize. This lack of knowledge is one device the devil uses to conceal his activity. One of the courses in our International School of Exorcism teaches that:

1. Seven of the 28 chapters of Matthew include references to demonic activity. In Matthew 10:1-6 the command to

"cast out demons," along with other miraculous acts, occurs without mention of the salvation message.

2. In Mark's Gospel seven of 16 chapters deal with the demonic. This Gospel includes the Great Commission of Mark 16:15-17 which tells us the most important sign of the Gospel's effectiveness is the "sign" of casting out demons.

3. In Luke, the third synoptic Gospel, eight of 24 chapters contain accounts of demonic encounters.

Fully one-third of the chapters of Matthew, Mark, and Luke refer to demonic possession and direct Christ's followers to cast out demons.

In his classic work, *In the Name of Jesus,* Graham H. Twelftree, Ph.D., of the University of Nottingham and distinguished professor of New Testament at the School of Divinity at Regent University, writes: "...all healing involves God's adversary being defeated. As exorcism was included in Luke's use of the phrase 'signs and wonders'...readers would assume that exorcism was included in the 'signs and wonders' of his [Luke's] followers" (page 134).

In this same section of his book, Twelftree goes on to say, "Also since exorcism and the kingdom of God were so closely tied in the ministry of Jesus, readers could assume that exorcism was involved when Luke says that the early Christians proclaimed the kingdom of God."

Having established that exorcism, the casting out of demons, has a foundational biblical basis, it then follows that what Scripture says about demons is equally important. The Bible is instructive about what demons do. Among their activities, taught in detail in our School of Exorcism, are purposes such as: afflicting believers (see Luke 13:16); destroying the work of God (see Mark 4:15); distorting Scripture (see Gen. 3:1); misusing God's Word (see Matt. 4:6); and many other evil machinations. We also know that demons cause physical disease (see Luke 13:16), muteness/deafness (see Mark 9:25), blindness (see Matt. 12:22), as well as states of handicap and various infirmities.

Occult literature and various texts of black magic and alchemy catalogue thousands of names of demons and arrange them in specific hierarchies of evil. Elaborate instructions are given on how to conjure these evil spirits and invoke their various depraved abilities. God's Word is a record of the Lord's dealings with humanity so there is no need to instruct readers with such information regarding the names and operations of all agents of evil. The Bible does, however, gives us some names of particular demons such as Lucifer, Satan, Beelzebub, Legion, Abaddon, Apollyon, Leviathan, Belial, Dragon, Serpent, Baal, and Moloch.

But one demon is unique. There is only once in the Bible that Christ directly referred to a particular demon as a matter of spiritual choice. Only once did Jesus juxtapose the name of a demon with the Kingdom of Heaven in terms of allegiance and fidelity. This demon whom Jezebel shields, worshiped in ancient times with the act of infanticide, sought and invoked through the ages as a source of power, sensuality, and wealth is the demon I encountered those three memorable days in Ukraine.

Christ referred to this demon in his Sermon on the Mount. Tucked away in chapters five, six, and seven of Matthew's Gospel is this instruction by Christ: "No one can serve two masters; for either he will hate the one and love the other, or else he will be loyal to the one and despise the other. You cannot serve God and mammon" (Matt. 6:24).

MAMMON!

MAMMON REVEALED

Mammon! The demon of avarice and all inordinate desire for gain and wealth at any cost. The demon of riches and greed. This is the demon declared by Christ as epitomizing the ultimate choice we all must make between Satan's kingdom and God's.

That night in a hotel room in Novomoskovsk, Ukraine I received a new revelation, an insight into the spirit world that had been hidden from even me: Jezebel, as ubiquitous and evil as she is, sometimes conceals an even more powerful demon. And this demon is the root cause of *all* evil that exists on the planet. Shocked? Have you forgotten the words of Paul's instruction to Timothy?—"For the love of money is a root of all kinds of evil" (1 Tim. 6:10).

This demon is everywhere in our culture. He is depicted in role-playing games, such as Dungeons & Dragons, and is prominent in Japanese cartoon anime graphics. He's a comic book character in the demonic *Spawn* (of Satan) series. To the ancient Syrians he was the god who promised plenty. To the Greeks he was Plutus, worshiped as the god of wealth. Like Jezebel, he has assumed many forms in many civilizations. He has appeared in ancient motifs as a wolf, bull, and as a crow. He is lust, injustice, craving, inordinate passion, unrighteous and ill-gained wealth. He is in Milton's *Paradise Lost* and in Dante's *Inferno*. He demands human blood and is often associated with Moloch and the sacrifice of the firstborn child. He is said to rule in Hades with the other Princes: Lucifer, Asmodeus, Satan, Beelzebub, Leviathan, and Belphegore.

Caution! Before you run to a Bible commentary to check out the origin and etymology of this name, be aware that most Bible scholars have little or no knowledge of spiritual warfare and conveniently explain away the references to this demon in Matthew 6:24. These writers will tell you that this passage refers to the ungodly pursuit of wealth, that "Mammon" is another way of saying "money." Granted, that is one way to understand the warning of Christ, but the words of Jesus in this case are not only figurative, they are literal. Christ is cautioning against a rapacious desire for possession, but he is also instructing us regarding the demon fueling those desires—*Mammon!* The choice is not just between the Creator and selfish worldly gain; our Lord is sending a message that there is a stark option that must be exercised by free will: *Choose God—or the demon Mammon!*

Overcoming Mammon

As important as this revelation is, it does not mean that every financial malady can be blamed on the curse of Mammon. Poverty and financial woes can result from many factors. Before you, the reader, point at demons as being responsible for your economic troubles, consider these factors that can cause money woes: mismanagement of finances with bad investments and unwise expenditures; living beyond your means due to greed and insecurity; the effect of societal economic conditions such as recessions or stock market drops; inadequate education or training that inhibits employment advancement; personal crises such as accidents, ill health, and even death of a wage earner. There are many factors affecting personal wealth. Satan may be behind some of your losses or lack, but you can't blame the devil when you have been profligate or unwise.

Keep in mind that financial curses by Mammon can be made worse by generational lust for wealth; by deals made by your ancestors to escape impoverishment; assignments of evil spirits to prevent you from supporting the work of God; and your lack of giving tithes and offerings for the work of the Lord and therefore bringing a curse on your own head (see Mal. 3:8–10).

Here is what's important to keep in mind: (1) To escape poverty and acquire wealth you need a multifaceted strategy that includes education, hard work, and wise investments; (2) You need to break the curses of Mammon because of your actions or the deeds of your ancestors.

Consequently, you need to put your house in order by: (1) Budgeting wisely and seeking financial counsel. (2) Getting out of debt, especially credit card debt. (3) Confessing any sins which may have led to the bondage of Mammon, such as purchasing pornography, gambling, or excessive expenditures on alcohol and drugs.

The promise of God's Word is this. As you "cheerfully give" (see 2 Cor. 9:7) then "God is able to make it up to you by giving you everything you need and more so that there will be enough for your own needs but plenty left over to give joyfully to others" (2 Cor. 9:8, TLB).

Get your financial house in order. Implement wise economic practices such as those suggested above. Pray to break all the ancestral curses of Mammon. Resist the spirit of Jezebel that hides this evil one.

Bind Jezebel to Mammon, and command, in the Name of Jesus, this tandem of iniquity to release you, all your loved ones, and all that you have from every bondage in any form. Jezebel and Mammon work hand-in-hand. Unless deliverance ministries have sufficient knowledge about the craftiness of Jezebel, who often shields Mammon, they will not push to the root of this demonic interloper. Get ready to experience freedom in your health, finances, relationships, worship, marriage, church, and every area of life. You *can* defeat your #1 spiritual enemy—*Jezebel!*

Jezebel-Proofing Prayer

Jezebel is a spirit, and she can only be defeated by confronting her spiritually through the power of prayer. But a Jezebel-proofing prayer can't be random. It must be specific. It must focus on the exact characteristics of this evil spirit. An important lesson that I've learned in waging spiritual warfare is that the more precise a prayer is in language and context, the more effective it is. For example, in breaking curses, the more you focus on the details, the more effectively the spiritual oppression is lifted. With this in mind, I've attempted to be as particular as possible to help you proof your life against every attack of the spirit of Jezebel.

PRAYER OF FREEDOM FROM
JEZEBEL AND MAMMON

In the Name of Jesus, and by the blood of Christ, I boldly confront the spirit of Jezebel. According to Ecclesiastes 4:12, I bind together with a threefold cord all evil spirits which are part of this kingdom of Jezebel. I resist you, Jezebel, by the power of Christ, He who was crucified and who rose again from the dead. Obey Him, you spirit of domination, treachery, illness, sickness, derangement, prevarication, deceit, lewdness, corruption, slaughter, suicide, coveting, cupidity, destitution, penury, indigence, divination, and the occult.

The wrath of God awaits you and all your kind, including Baal, Moloch, Lust, Death, Murder, Witchcraft, Mammon, and Lucifer. Fear and obey Christ who was crucified for sin and triumphed over the all the powers of hell. You, Jezebel, along with all your evil angels, have been cast from the heights of Heaven, and by the grace of God's Lamb you shall be cast down to the depths of the Abyss.

I resist you by the grace of my Lord Jesus Christ and expel you from every province of my spirit, body, and soul, according to the command of my Savior, who promised that those who believe in Him would trample on serpents and scorpions. Despite my unworthiness in the flesh, I confront you in the Spirit of Him who dwells in me; He who walked on water, calmed the waves, opened blind eyes, healed sick bodies, and called forth the dead from the grave. You, Jezebel, are nothing in His sight, merely an instigator of evil and vice, pain and sorrow.

I confront you in each of your identities and actions, every transmutation, transformation, and permutation. I lay bare all your disguises, fraudulence, and trickery. Be judged now for all you have done to me and my ancestors, back to Adam and Eve and every progenitor in between. Every vow and oath made on your behalf is renounced. Every ritual and ceremony performed for you and your minions is annulled. Every blood covenant executed at your instigation is canceled. All acts of violence, murder, rape, abuse, molestation, adultery, fornication, perversion, and uncleanness done in your name are voided.

Each attempt by you to discredit the Christian Church, and all those faithful who serve Him by calling and ordination, *will no longer be tolerated. You, Jezebel, must end now every effort to destroy any and all valid relationships I have entered into by the Lord's will. This includes all friendships, all kinships by blood or marriage, and my spousal covenant (if married).*

Every contract and agreement ratified on your behalf by my ancestors is revoked. All curses instigated by you and agreed to by my forebears are hereby broken.

Having made this declaration before the powers of hell and the angels of Heaven, you, Jezebel, must now completely and entirely release me from all of your assignments and hereditary obligations that lead to the following:

- *Control and manipulation*
- *Infirmity and disease*
- *Lies and deceit*
- *Lust and seduction*
- *Murder and death*
- *Greed and avarice*
- *Poverty and lack*
- *Witchcraft and sorcery*

Depart now forever, Jezebel, from me and my descendants. All your curses, all your assignments, all your treacheries are now and forever disannulled. I declare that inasmuch as Mammon may not be speaking for himself, you speak for him and all his treasonous acts before Almighty God.

Mammon, release now all the hindrances you have placed to prevent my godly prosperity and the fruit of my labors. Remove all sicknesses you have put upon my body to rob me of health and happiness. Take away every scheme to steal my right to gainful employment and personal enrichment that I may bless and sustain the work of God. Every accord of my ancestors that was made to derive from you power, sensual gratification, or unmerited wealth, is now of no effect. I particularly reject those agreements invoked by human or animal sacrifice. All such offerings are abolished by the covenant of Christ through his sacrificial, blood atonement on the cross. Furthermore, by the law of restitution you, Jezebel, and Mammon, will restore sevenfold what has been stolen from me and those dear to me. All your curses and covenants must come to an end, now!

I loose the dogs of Jezreel to speedily come and eat your flesh and lick your blood, Jezebel. I call upon the horses of Jehu to trample you in terror and judgment. There will be no mercy for you, Jezebel and Mammon, nor to all your subordinates. You are foul and despicable agents of evil, likewise deserving of the punishment due that fallen angel Lucifer with whom you conspired in rebellion.

By the power of the incarnation, the crucifixion, and the resurrection of my Lord, begone, taking with you all your artifices of evil and the craftiness of your wicked schemes. Never return again to beguile me or my descendants with your lure of ill-gotten gains and pleasures. Never again will your deception cause my bloodline to be taken captive.

I am free from you, Jezebel.

I am free from you, Mammon.

I am free to receive all the blessings of my inheritance as a redeemed child of God.

I am free now and until I am present with Christ who prepares a place for me with Him.

All praise be to Him who lives and reigns forever at the right hand of the Father.

All this I declare in the Name of the Father, the Son, and the Holy Spirit.

Amen.

ABOUT THE AUTHOR

REV. BOB LARSON IS THE WORLD'S FOREMOST EXPERT ON CULTS, THE occult, and supernatural phenomena. He has ministered in more than 100 countries and has appeared on TV networks and shows such as *The Oprah Winfrey Show,* CNBC, *Larry King Live, The O'Reilly Factor, Inside Edition,* Entertainment Tonight, *The Insider,* CNN's *The Anderson Cooper Show,* ABC-TV's *Good Morning America,* ABC-TV's *Nightline, A Current Affair, Politically Incorrect,* MSNBC, *CNN Headline News, Hannity, Geraldo at Large,* and *Dr. Phil.* Numerous television networks have produced documentaries about Bob, including Discovery, Showtime, TLC, A&E, BBC, History, National Geographic, and MSNBC. Bob has been featured in *The Los Angeles Times, The New York Times, The Washington Post, Financial Times, Glamour, Marie Claire,* and other major publications. International Network TV reports have included Brazil, Germany, Norway, France, Australia, New Zealand, Canada, Holland, Belgium, Japan, and others. Bob is also the author of 34 books, including *Larson's Book of Spiritual Warfare, Larson's Book of World Religions, Demon Proofing Prayers, Curse Breaking,* and four nonfiction novels.

Get Free. Stay Free. Live Free.
with Pastor Bob Larson

The world's foremost expert on cults, the occult, and supernatural phenomena, Bob has spoken in more than 100 countries and written 34 books translated into more than a dozen languages.

Personal Spiritual Encounter

Fulfill your spiritual destiny, and get the life you've always wanted.

Let Bob help you overcome obstacles holding you back.

THE REAL EXORCIST

youtube.com/boblarsonexorcism

See Bob unmask and confront demons on YouTube.

Every week Bob answers questions about demons and exorcisms.

Do YOU Have a Demon?

Diagnose your spiritual life with Bob's comprehensive online test.

International School of Exorcism

Enroll in Bob's online school today to become a Spiritual Warrior. Learn how to defeat the Forces of Darkness.

See Bob in Your Area.
Call 303-980-1511, or go to boblarson.org.

Spiritual Freedom Church
Luke 4:18